I0620165

HEROES AND HEAVIES OF THE APOCRYPHA

DISCOVER LIFE-CHANGING SPIRITUAL INSIGHTS FROM 100 INTRIGUING CHARACTERS

BIBLE CHARACTER SKETCHES SERIES
BOOK 5

PETER DEHAAN

Library of Congress Control Number: 2024910443

Published by Rock Rooster Books, Grand Rapids, Michigan

ISBNs:

- 979-8-88809-086-2 (e-book)
- 979-8-88809-087-9 (paperback)
- 979-8-88809-088-6 (hardcover)

Credits:

- Developmental editor: Julie Harbison
- Copy editor: Robyn Mulder
- Cover design: Cassidy Wierks
- Author photo: Chelsie Jensen Photography

To Patricia M. Robertson

Series by Peter DeHaan

Bible Character Sketches Series celebrates people in Scripture, from the well-known to the obscure.

Holiday Celebration Bible Study Series rejoices in the holidays with Jesus.

Visiting Churches Series takes an in-person look at church practices and traditions to inform and inspire today's followers of Jesus.

40–Day Bible Study Series takes a fresh and practical look into Scripture, book by book.

Be the first to hear about Peter's new books and receive updates at PeterDeHaan.com/updates.

CONTENTS

Celebrating the Apocrypha   1

Tobit   5

1: Tobit   7
2: Anna (2)   10
3: Deborah (3)   12
4: Gabael (2)   14
5: Sarah (2)   16
6: Azariah (24) (Raphael)   18
7: Raguel (2)   22
8: Edna   24
9: Tobias   26
10: Ahikar   29
11: Nadab   31

Judith   33

12: Arphaxad (1)   35
13: Holofernes   37
14: Joakim (3)   40
15: Achior   42
16: Uzziah (7)   45
17: Chabris and Charmis   48
18: Bagoas   50
19: Manasseh (5)   52
20: Judith (2)   54

Greek Esther   59

21: Gabatha and Tharra   63

22: Artaxerxes 65
23: Vashti 67
24: Memucan 70
25: Haman 72
26: Mordecai (1) 74
27: Zeresh 76
28: Hegai 78
29: Shaashgaz 80
30: Esther 82
31: Ten Sons of Haman 85
32: Dositheus (2) 87

Wisdom 89

33: Solomon 91

Sirach 93

34: Simon (11) 95
35: Jesus (4) 97

Baruch 99

36: Baruch (1) 101
37: Jeconiah 103
38: Belshazzar 105

Letter of Jeremiah 109

39: Jeremiah 111

Prayer Of Azariah 113

40: Azariah (23) 115
41: Hananiah, Mishael, and Azariah 117

Susanna 121

42: Joakim (1)   123
43: Two Elders   125
44: Susanna   127
45: Daniel   129
46: Hilkiah (14)   132

Bel and the Dragon   135

47: Cyrus   137
48: Bel   139
49: The Dragon   142
(Daniel, Part 2)   144
50: Habakkuk   146

1 Maccabees   149

51: Darius   151
52: Alexander (6)   153
53: Antiochus (1)   155
54: Mattathias (1)   158
55: John (7) (Gaddi)   161
56: Azariah (25)   163
57: Judas (7) Maccabeus   165
58: Lysias   167
59: Eleazar (9) (Avaran)   169
60: Ptolemy (1)   171
61: Cleopatra   173
62: Demetrius (4)   175
63: Jonathan (9) (Apphus)   177
64: Simon (12) (Thassi)   179
65: Mattathias (2) and Judas (9)   181
66: John (9)   183

2 Maccabees   185

67: Jason of Cyrene   187

68: Simon (13)   189
69: Heliodorus   191
70: Menelaus   194
71: Jason (5)   196
72: Auranus   198
73: Philip (6)   200
74: Antiochus Epiphanes   202
75: Nicanor   204
76: Razis   207

1 Esdras   209

77: Josiah   211
78: Jehoiakim   213
79: Hilkiah (11)   215
80: Nebuchadnezzar   217
81: Zedekiah   220
82: Sheshbazzar   222
83: Zerubbabel   224
84: Jeshua (3)   226
85: Nehemiah   228
86: Haggai and Zechariah (15)   230

Prayer of Manasseh   233

87: Manasseh (2)   235

Psalm 151   237

88: David   239

3 Maccabees   241

89: Dositheus (1)   243
90: Ptolemy (4) Philopator   245
91: Simon (14)   247

92: Hermon   249
93: Eleazar (12)   251

2 Esdras   253

94: Uriel   255
95: Ezra   257
96: My Son   260

4 Maccabees   263

97: Onias   265
98: Apollonius (1)   267
99: Eleazar (13)   270
100: Seven Brothers and Their
Mother   273
Heroes, Heavies, and Us   275

Which Book Do You Want to Read Next?   278
About the Apocrypha   279
Duplicate Names   281
*For Small Groups, Sunday Schools, and
Classes*   301
If You're New to the Bible   303
About Peter DeHaan   306
Peter DeHaan's Books   308

CELEBRATING THE APOCRYPHA

The Apocrypha is a group of books found in some Bibles, but not most. Some Christians dismiss the Apocrypha. They think since it isn't in their Bible, then it doesn't matter.

They assume the Apocrypha was added to Scripture. In truth, it was deleted.

The Apocrypha was in the original King James Version but was later removed.

The Apocrypha was also part of the Septuagint, a Greek translation of Scripture in widespread use during Jesus's time. Jesus quoted from the Septuagint and so did the New Testament writers, including Paul.

Paul surely had the Apocrypha in mind (along

with what we now call the Old Testament) when he said that every Scripture is inspired by God and useful to educate and equip us (2 Timothy 3:16–17). *Every Scripture* means all parts—not some or just the parts in our Bible today. (Although the New Testament didn't exist when Paul wrote this, we add the New Testament books to our understanding of *every* Scripture.)

To celebrate and embrace the Apocrypha as part of *every* Scripture, we'll explore its many intriguing characters, both the good and the bad, the heroes and heavies. In doing so, we'll use as our basis the Common English Bible (CEB).

Here are the books of the Apocrypha as listed in the CEB:

- Tobit
- Judith
- Greek Esther
- Wisdom
- Sirach
- Baruch
- Letter of Jeremiah
- Prayer of Azariah
- Susanna
- Bel and the Dragon

- 1 Maccabees
- 2 Maccabees
- 1 Esdras
- Prayer of Manasseh
- Psalm 151
- 3 Maccabees
- 2 Esdras
- 4 Maccabees

Though this isn't chronological, we'll follow this order (as published in the CEB) for our discussion. This makes it easy to follow along in the CEB. In addition, some Apocryphal books are challenging to place on a timeline, as with other Old Testament books, such as Joel.

Many of the books in the Apocrypha contain history, but we'd be wrong to scrutinize them for historical details. Instead, our focus should rest on the narrative and the spiritual lessons we can learn from it.

Sometimes, references to historical people or nations may be archetypes instead of literal. This technique occurs throughout the Bible.

For example, the Bible continues to use the label of *Israel* after the nation's destruction, applying it metaphorically to the nation of Judah or generically to all remaining Hebrew people. *Son of David* sometimes refers to David's biological sons, such as Amnon, Absalom, or Solomon. But it can also refer to Jesus, one of David's distant descendants.

Discover more in the "About the Apocrypha" section at the end of this book. Also, note that several people share names with other biblical characters. Whenever we encounter a duplicate name, we'll add a numerical suffix to help us keep them straight. See the "Duplicate Names" section in this book's back matter.

How do you view the Apocrypha? Do you know of any characters in the Apocrypha? If so, who?

[Discover more in Acts 17:11.]

TOBIT

Tobit is from the tribe of Naphtali. When Assyria defeats Israel, they deport many of the people. Tobit ends up in the city of Nineveh. Tobit is a key character and the author of this book, which is named after him. Yet the account primarily revolves around the adventures of his son Tobias.

At the request of his father, Tobias travels to a distant city to collect some silver his dad put on deposit with a relative. Tobias travels with a hired companion to guide him.

Their journey is an epic adventure. Not only do they successfully retrieve the silver, but Tobias gets married along the way, defeats a demon, and brings his bride home.

He also has something special for his father.

1: TOBIT

Tobit is a righteous man. He follows the tithes Moses prescribed and goes to Jerusalem to worship as the law commands. He does this even though the other people from his tribe of Naphtali and the rest of Israel do not.

When Assyria conquers Israel, they deport many of the people. This includes Tobit. He ends up in Nineveh, where he works on behalf of King Shalmaneser. He continues to give food to the hungry and clothes to those in need. In secret, he also respectfully buries any of his fellow Jews when they are murdered.

When his covert activities become known, he

flees for his life. All his possessions and wealth are seized. Later, his nephew works on his behalf to allow him to return, restoring his wife and son—Anna and Tobias—to him. But his confiscated property is not returned. He has nothing. He is now poor.

Despite all that's happened, Tobit continues to bury his fellow Jews who have been murdered. He does this even though his neighbors mock him for it. Soon after this, he becomes blind. Despondent, he wants to die. He prays God will take him, freeing him from the torment of life to bring him into eternity.

Tobit gives final instructions to his son Tobias, encouraging him to live a righteous life, help those in need, and marry a woman from among their people. He also tells Tobias about 570 pounds of silver he entrusted to their relative Gabael and tells his son to travel there to reclaim it.

Tobit gives his son a receipt for the silver. He arranges for Azariah to travel with Tobias as a guide and implicitly for protection, because the road is dangerous.

What can we do to help the poor like Tobit did? When we have little to give, are we willing to share a portion of it with those in need?

[Read about Tobit in Tobit 1:3–9 and Tobit 3:1–6. Discover more about helping others in Deuteronomy 26:12.]

2: ANNA (2)

Anna is the wife of Tobit and the mother of Tobias. She makes a living weaving cloth out of wool. Since her husband is now blind, there's nothing he can do to earn a living.

One time, Anna receives a goat as a bonus for her work. Tobit hears the bleating animal and accuses her of stealing it. He doesn't believe her when she says she earned it. He grows angry at her, and she mocks him.

When Tobit sends Tobias off to retrieve their silver, Anna despairs. She fears he will not return. After he doesn't come back in a reasonable time, she assumes he is dead. Even so, she diligently watches for him to return.

We can applaud Anna for working to support her husband when he cannot. We can also celebrate the quality of her work, for she earns a bonus for her labor. Yet she also worries about her son's fate and assumes the worst has happened.

Whether or not we receive a bonus, is our work worthy of one? When have we let our imagination take over and assumed the worst?

[Read about Anna in Tobit 2:11–14 and Tobit 10:4–7. Discover another person who made a wrong assumption in Genesis 37:32–34.]

3: DEBORAH (3)

Deborah is the grandmother of Tobit. She raised him when his father died and left him as an orphan. Most importantly, she taught him.

We see the results of her teaching when we look at the righteous way Tobit lived and how he did what was right and cared for those in need. His actions result from his grandmother's instructions when he was young.

In this way, she played an indirect part in helping others throughout the years. And this legacy continues beyond her life, for the rest of her grandson's.

Who can benefit from our instruction today? What legacy are we leaving for our family to carry on?

[Read about Deborah in Tobit 1:8. Discover the influence of another grandmother in 2 Timothy 1:5.]

4: GABAEL (2)

Gabael lives in Rages of Media. Tobit often travels to Media to conduct business for King Shalmaneser. On one of his trips, he entrusts 570 pounds of silver with Gabael, his relative.

They each execute a document about the transaction. Tearing them in two, each man keeps one half. In this way, anyone who presents Gabael with Tobit's half of the document can receive the silver. This will work well for Tobit's son Tobias, since he doesn't know who Gabael is and Gabael has never met Tobias.

After Shalmaneser dies, the roads to Media become too dangerous for safe travel, and Tobit can no longer go there. This means he has no way of retrieving his silver from Gabael.

Gabael faithfully holds on to the silver, even though he hasn't heard from Tobit in over twenty years.

Can other people entrust us with their property? Are we dependable to carry out all that we promise to do?

[Read about Gabael in Tobit 1:14 and Tobit 9:6. Discover another interesting transaction in Jeremiah 32:6–15.]

5: SARAH (2)

Sarah is the daughter of Raguel and Edna, their only child. She is sensible; she is courageous; and she is gorgeous.

She's also been married seven times. This doesn't reflect her character, however, but her circumstances. On her wedding night, before the couple can consummate their union, a demon kills the groom. This happens with each of her seven marriages. But the demon never harms Sarah because he loves her (see Genesis 6:1–2).

One of Sarah's servants accuses her of killing all seven men. This is surely something other people have suspected as well and may have even said to her. Distraught, Sarah plans to hang herself.

She reaches her decision the same day Tobit asks God to take his life.

But Sarah realizes that committing suicide will disgrace her father. She doesn't want to bring him sorrow. Instead, she begs God to let her die. Then she'll no longer have to endure the insults of those who think she killed all seven of her husbands.

Death seems like the only solution to her torment.

When have we despaired of life? Have we ever considered death as the solution to our problems?

[Read about Sarah in Tobit 3:7–15 and Tobit 6:10–18. Discover another person who despaired of life in Job 3:1–3.]

6: AZARIAH (24) (RAPHAEL)

Azariah reveals himself as a distant relative of Tobit. He knows well the road to Media, having traveled it many times. He's even stayed with their relative Raguel along the way. Azariah is quick to agree to accompany Tobias on this journey to retrieve the silver from Gabael.

Tobit blesses the pair, and they head out. What a remarkable adventure it is!

On their first day of travel, they reach the Tigris River and camp there. As Tobias washes his feet in the river, a huge fish jumps from the water and tries to take a bite out of his foot. Azariah tells Tobias to grab the fish and hold on.

Once caught, Azariah instructs Tobias to

remove the fish's gallbladder, heart, and liver for medicinal purposes. The gallbladder can heal a person's eyes, while the heart and liver can chase away demons.

The next day, they continue their journey and travel to Ecbatana of Media, where their relative Raguel lives. Azariah reminds Tobias of Raguel's daughter, Sarah. Tobias is the next closest relative to marry her (see Leviticus 25:25 and Ruth 3:12–13).

Tobias knows about her seven prior husbands who each died on their wedding night. He doesn't want to be number eight.

Yet Azariah reminds Tobias of his father's instruction to not marry a foreign woman and instead find a bride from their own people. Besides, he has a plan and tells Tobias not to worry. Though he's not yet met Sarah, Tobias falls in love with her.

Tobit, Anna, Tobias, Gabael, Raguel, Sarah, and Edna (whom we'll meet in a bit) all know Tobias's companion as Azariah, but his real name is Raphael. He's an angel in disguise. Yet he keeps his angelic identity a secret—for now. Raphael is one of seven angels who stand in God's presence. As such, he must be an important one. We can wonder if this makes him an archangel, like Michael (Jude 1:9).

Back when Tobit and Sarah had both prayed to God, asking him to take their lives, God sent Raphael to help them. Traveling with Tobias to retrieve his father's silver and staying with Raguel is part of his plan.

At Raphael's urging, Tobias asks Raguel for permission to marry Sarah. After warning Tobias of her past seven marriages—each ending with the groom's death—Raguel agrees.

On their wedding night, Tobias burns the fish's heart and liver over the incense coals as Raphael had instructed. The smell drives the demon away, and Raphael chases him to Egypt, where he subdues him and binds him in chains. Tobias is safe.

The next day, Raguel and his wife, Edna, are relieved to learn that Tobias lived through the night. They hold a fourteen-day wedding celebration for the couple.

Through Raphael, God answered Sarah's prayer for deliverance. Though it didn't work out the way she intended, God's way was much better.

When has God answered our prayers in a way that exceeded our expectations? How should we react to the idea of God sending his angels—be it physically or spiritually—to help us?

[Read about Azariah in Tobit 5:4–17 and Tobit 6. Read about Raphael in Tobit 12:11–18. Discover more about angels in Hebrews 13:2 and another supernatural confrontation in Revelation 20:1–3.]

7: RAGUEL (2)

Raguel lives in Ecbatana of Media. His wife is Edna, and their daughter is Sarah, whose seven husbands all died on their wedding nights.

When Tobias asks Raguel to marry Sarah, he's apprehensive. He reminds Tobias of what happened to his daughter's prior husbands. Tobias persists, and they sign a marriage contract. That evening, Tobias enters Sarah's bedroom to consummate their union.

Assuming the worst, that night Raguel takes some servants and digs a grave for Tobias. That way, they can bury him quickly before anyone finds out that Sarah lost an eighth husband.

Yet before dawn, a female servant checks on the

couple and finds Tobias is still alive. Raguel sends his servants to fill the burial site before it gets light, lest people see the unused grave.

Raguel holds a fourteen-day wedding celebration, while Raphael goes with four servants and two camels to receive the silver from Gabael. Gabael even returns with Raphael to join the feast.

Raguel, Edna, and Gabael all praise God for Tobias and Sarah's marriage. Yet Sarah has the biggest reason to celebrate. The demon that killed her prior husbands is gone, and she at last has a husband who lived through the night.

Like Raguel, when have we warned someone about something that didn't occur? When have we reacted to a worry that never materialized?

[Read about Raguel in Tobit 7 and Tobit 8:9–19. Discover when Jacob worried about losing Benjamin in Genesis 43:14.]

8: EDNA

E dna is the wife of Raguel and the mother of Sarah.

When Sarah marries for the eighth time, Edna prepares the bridal chamber for her daughter and future son-in-law. She weeps. Are these tears of joy or tears of sorrow? Likely both.

As with any mother of the bride, Edna is certainly joyful over the wedding of her only daughter. Yet she's been here before—seven times. So her tears are also for the anguish her daughter will feel when her groom most likely dies.

Sarah probably cries as well—and for the same two reasons.

Yet Edna is optimistic. She encourages her daughter and tells Sarah to be courageous. She blesses Sarah with joy to replace the pain she feels over seven dead husbands. "Take courage, my daughter." Then Edna leaves.

Her blessing holds true. Tobias survives the night, and Sarah at last emerges from her bridal chamber with a husband who is alive.

Two weeks later, as the newlyweds are about to set off for Tobias's home, Edna entrusts Sarah to Tobias's care. She sends them off in peace with the affirming statement to Tobias, "From now on, I am your mother."

In doing so, Edna embraces Tobias as her own son, in effect adopting him into their family. Though her daughter—her only child—is about to leave home, Edna isn't losing a daughter. She's gaining a son.

Do we view marriage as losing or gaining? When faced with fear, do we react positively and proclaim blessing on what will be?

[Read about Edna in Tobit 7:15–16 and Tobit 10:12. Discover more about being adopted in Galatians 4:4–6.]

9: TOBIAS

Tobias is the son of Tobit and Anna. Though this book in Scripture carries his father's name, Tobias stands as its central character. The lives of all the other people intersect with his.

We already know that Tobias's father goes blind and despairs of living. He sends his son on a trek to reclaim a stockpile of silver held by a relative. They hire a man to guide Tobias, but he's really an angel in disguise.

Four key things occur on their journey:

First, when a fish attacks Tobias, the angel tells him to seize it and remove the fish's gallbladder, heart, and liver. The gallbladder can restore sight, while the heart and liver can repel demons.

Next, Tobias marries Sarah. This is despite that she's seven times a widow from a demon killing each husband on their wedding night.

Third, on their wedding night, Tobias burns the fish heart and liver. This chases away the demon.

Last, while Tobias and Sarah celebrate their wedding, the angel travels on to retrieve the silver.

Once the marriage celebration ends, Tobias and Sarah head to his home. They take with them the silver, along with half of her parents' wealth as a wedding gift. When they arrive, Tobias uses the fish gallbladder to restore his father's sight. The newlyweds have another wedding celebration, as well as marking Tobias's safe return and Tobit's healing.

Tobit lives another fifty years, but before he dies, he prophesies about the future and tells Tobias to leave Nineveh as soon as his mother dies.

Then Tobias and Sarah move to her family, where he takes care of his in-laws for the rest of their lives.

Tobias lives to be 117. His steadfast obedience to his father and to the angel who guided him mark his life. Along the way, we celebrate with him God's supernatural provisions.

If we have a guide or a mentor, do we always do as they instruct? Do we expect God's supernatural provisions in our lives?

[Read about Tobias in Tobit 11:10–17 and Tobit 14:12–14. Discover more about when Jesus heals a blind man in John 9:1–7.]

10: AHIKAR

Ahikar is one of Tobit's nephews, the son of his brother Hanael. His name shows up five times throughout the book of Tobit.

When Esarhaddon becomes king, he hires Ahikar to oversee his finances and records. Ahikar also keeps the king's signet ring and becomes second in command. This reveals Ahikar's trustworthy character.

When Tobit flees for his life, Ahikar intercedes on his behalf before the king to bring about Tobit's return. And after Tobit becomes blind, Ahikar cares for him.

The other two mentions of Ahikar in the book

of Tobit relate to his brother (or cousin) Nadab, whom we'll cover shortly.

How trustworthy is our character? Regardless of the outcome, do we conduct ourselves worthy of serving in responsible positions?

[Read about Ahikar in Tobit 1:21–22 and Tobit 2:10. Discover other trustworthy men in 2 Kings 22:4–7.]

11: NADAB

Like Ahikar, Nadab is also a nephew of Tobit. Given the context, we can assume Ahikar and Nadab are brothers, but at the very least, they're cousins. Besides caring for Tobit in his blindness, Ahikar had also raised Nadab.

When Tobias returns home with his bride, both Ahikar and Nadab join the celebration, rejoicing with the happy couple.

Yet some fifty years later, as Tobit nears death, he makes a curious statement about Nadab. He reminds Tobias what Nadab did and to be mindful of it.

Though we don't know his motivation, at some point, Nadab attempted to kill Ahikar. In doing so,

Nadab fell into a death trap that destroys him, ushering him into eternal darkness.

How do we react when someone we helped turns against us? What is our reaction to the idea of eternal darkness?

[Read about Nadab in Tobit 11:18 and Tobit 14:10. Discover more about utter darkness in Isaiah 8:21–22.]

JUDITH

The book of Judith is another epic tale. It tells us about a wise and beautiful woman, full of faith and piety, who trusts God to use her to save her people from annihilation.

It's an encouraging lesson of how one person—along with God—can accomplish amazing things in the most hopeless of situations. Yes, with God guiding us, one person can make a difference.

Though this book bears her name, we don't meet Judith until halfway through. So be patient as we establish the framework and enjoy the setup.

12: ARPHAXAD (1)

The book of Judith opens with what reads like a prologue. Prologues establish the framework for what follows, but often the characters in the prologue don't factor into the primary story. Such is the case with Arphaxad.

Arphaxad is the ruler of the Medes. His home base is Ecbatana. (Ecbatana, incidentally, is where Raguel lived. Tobias stopped there on his journey, and it is where he married Raguel's daughter, Sarah.)

In Ecbatana, Arphaxad builds an impressive fortification around the city using stones that are four and a half feet wide and nine feet long. He uses them to construct walls one hundred feet high and seventy-five feet wide. It's a formidable fortress.

Yet, it's not safe enough.

Intent on conquering Arphaxad and the Medes, Nebuchadnezzar battles against them. Though it takes five years, he prevails. He defeats Arphaxad's armies and kills Arphaxad.

Arphaxad trusted in his seemingly impregnable stronghold, but it wasn't strong enough.

What do we put our trust in? Are we wrong to strive for physical safety?

[Read about Arphaxad in Judith 1:1–6 and Judith 1:13–15. Discover other people who thought they were safe in 1 Thessalonians 5:1–3.]

13: HOLOFERNES

King Nebuchadnezzar sends his general, Holofernes, on a monumental mission of revenge. When the king had asked for the nations to the west of him for their help in defeating his enemies, they snubbed him. Having achieved victory, he now seeks revenge on those nations who dismissed him. Nebuchadnezzar sends his second in command, General Holofernes, to accomplish this goal.

Holofernes heads out with a formidable army of 120,000 infantry and 12,000 cavalry, along with baggage handlers and provisions.

As instructed, he ruthlessly destroys the peoples before him. Some nations hear of his conquests and seek peace. He doesn't subdue them and lets them live, but he also makes them subject to him and King Nebuchadnezzar.

The Jews living in the region—who just returned from captivity—don't seek peace. Having reinstituted worship in Jerusalem, they want to protect the temple and the altar from destruction by a foreign power. They put God first and prepare for war.

Enraged, Holofernes is determined to make them pay for their defiance.

The city of Bethulia, with its narrow mountain passes, stands as the gateway into Judea and Jerusalem. Holofernes lays siege to Bethulia. He plans to starve them into submission.

Yet, as ruthless as Holofernes is in dealing with the nations and people before him, he also shows an honorable side. When a beautiful woman—from the town he wants to destroy—comes before him, he treats her with respect. Though he desires her, he doesn't force himself upon her, even though he could. He has both the physical strength and the positional power to do whatever he wants. Instead, he desires to seduce her and patiently waits.

As such, Holofernes emerges as an enigma. Part of him is cruel. The other part is patient and honorable. Yet being partly good is not good enough.

Do others see us as an enigma? What must we do to have all aspects of our lives align with the faith we profess?

[Read about Holofernes in Judith 2:14–28, Judith 4:1–7, Judith 11:1–4, and Judith 12:10–19. Discover a man who was not patient and honorable in 2 Samuel 13:12–14.]

14: JOAKIM (3)

Joakim is the high priest in Jerusalem. Without being a nation or having a king, he leads the Jewish people in Judea. Not only is he their spiritual leader, but he also serves as their government leader too.

Seeing the threat before them, he writes to the people of Bethulia. He instructs them to guard the mountain passes, which are the access point into the region of Judea, where God's people live. The mountain passes are narrow, allowing only two men to pass through at a time. As such, they are easy to guard.

The people in Bethulia do as Joakim instructed.

The Jews throughout the land humble themselves before God, praying and fasting. They don funeral clothes and put ashes on their heads.

They don't want their families carried off, their cities destroyed, and their sanctuary defiled.

All this will happen if Holofernes succeeds in his mission of destruction.

Joakim leads wisely—both spiritually and strategically—to prevent this from happening. He gives practical advice for what the people can do and leads the people to seek God to handle the rest.

How do we react when faced with a formidable challenge? When confronting obstacles, do we react with a God-honoring confidence?

[Read about Joakim in Judith 4:6–15 and Judith 15:8. Discover three men who faced a formidable situation in Daniel 3:16–18.]

15: ACHIOR

Achior, leader of the Ammonites and mercenaries in Holofernes's army, comes to the general with wise advice. He tells the general and his advisors about the people they're intent on destroying. As a foreigner, his retelling of their history is most insightful.

Though he may have a slightly different historical twist on their past than how we understand it today, his summary is without flaw. When the people sin, God punishes them. When they don't sin, God prospers them.

Achior concludes by saying that if the people have sinned, they'll be easy to conquer. Yet if they have steadfastly obeyed God, he will protect them, and the best choice is to pass them by.

For his candor and astute recommendation, Holofernes and his advisers ridicule Achior. They attack him because they don't agree with his analysis. They see him as foolish and them as invincible.

As punishment, they send him to the people of Bethulia so that he'll suffer along with them and die when they do. His only chance at living is if Holofernes fails, and that won't happen.

Holofernes's slaves take Achior as close to Bethulia as they can safely get. They tie him to a tree and abandon him.

The people of Bethulia find Achior and bring him into the town. He tells them what happened and of Holofernes's boast of what he plans to do to them.

The people fall and worship God. They pray, begging him for mercy and favor. And they comfort Achior.

When have we received criticism for telling the truth or offering sound advice? Alternatively, when have we been quiet out of fear when we should have spoken?

[Read about Achior in Judith 5:5–6:20 and Judith 14:10. Discover more about telling the truth in Galatians 4:16.]

16: UZZIAH (7)

Uzziah is one of Bethulia's rulers—or elders—along with Chabris and Charmis. Since Uzziah's name always appears first, we can assume he is the lead elder. That's how he acts. Perhaps he's like a city mayor.

After Achior tells the people of Bethulia all that happened and of Holofernes's threats—to their city, to the Jews living in the area, and to their way of life—Uzziah takes Achior to his own house and gives a feast for the elders. Throughout the night, they call on God for deliverance.

Holofernes begins his siege of the city the next morning.

After thirty-four days, the people can't take any

more. They've suffered long enough. They're hungry, thirsty, and impatient. Questioning his leadership, they come to Uzziah and demand action.

Claiming there is no one to help them, they beg him to surrender to Holofernes. They'd rather have their city plundered and to live as slaves than to suffer any longer.

Uzziah doesn't directly give in to their demands, nor does he stand up against them. He offers a compromise. He asks them to wait five more days for God to rescue them. If the five days come and go without the Lord's help, Uzziah will surrender the city to Holofernes.

Though Uzziah doesn't completely yield to the people's will, he also doesn't completely place his confidence in God. Instead, he gives God a deadline.

Uzziah's trust in supernatural deliverance isn't absolute. It's iffy.

When have we given God a deadline? When have we vacillated between public opinion and staying true to the Lord?

[Read about Uzziah in Judith 6:14–21, Judith 7:23–32, and Judith 15:4. Discover another ruler who gave in to pressure from others in 1 Samuel 13:8–14.]

17: CHABRIS AND CHARMIS

Along with Uzziah, Chabris and Charmis are elders in the city of Bethulia. Chabris's and Charmis's names always appear in tandem, and they always follow Uzziah.

Though all three men are elders, Uzziah takes the lead in running the city. Though Chabris and Charmis are present, they're also passive. They appear as figureheads and nothing more.

The text never mentions them discussing the situation with Uzziah or offering him their opinions. Yet, as elders who say nothing, they implicitly endorse what Uzziah says and does.

When have we been passive when we should have been active? What do we endorse with our silence?

[Read about Chabris and Charmis in Judith 6:15, Judith 8:10, and Judith 10:6. Discover another man who says nothing in Genesis 34:5.]

18: BAGOAS

Bagoas is a eunuch in the service of General Holofernes.

A eunuch can serve ably as an aide to a king or leader since he isn't susceptible to seduction. A eunuch is also trustworthy to oversee a harem since he can't give in to temptation. Though a eunuch seems like an ineffectual man, his close standing behind potent authorities provides him with much influence and insider knowledge.

Such is the case with Bagoas.

Bagoas serves Holofernes as a trusted aide who handles key elements of the general's life, but he does so as an almost invisible presence. Yet Holofernes depends on Bagoas to manage issues in his stead.

Though Bagoas seems like an inconsequential person, his behind-the-scenes work puts him in the middle of all the general's interactions. He looks after Holofernes's property, provides for his needs, and determines who has access.

In this way, Bagoas controls much.

If God calls us to serve in the background, are we content to do so? Do we strive to lead when we might better support an existing leader?

[Read about Bagoas in Judith 12:10–15 and Judith 13:1–3. Discover more about eunuchs in Matthew 19:12.]

19: MANASSEH (5)

Manasseh is a wealthy man. He's married to Judith. They're both from the tribe of Simeon. The Bible doesn't mention them having any children, and the context suggests they're childless.

During the barley harvest, Manasseh suffers from heat stroke. He returns home to Bethulia to recuperate but later dies in his bed.

This leaves Judith as a widow. Though Manasseh is not present to care for his wife, he leaves her well provided for. This includes gold, silver, slaves, cattle, and fields.

How can we best provide for our families both now and in the future? Whether our life is short or long, what should we do to make sure it matters?

[Read about Manasseh in Judith 8:2–7 and Judith 16:22–24. Discover more about widows in 1 Timothy 5:3–16.]

20: JUDITH (2)

Judith is a widow whose wealthy husband, Manasseh, left her well provided for. Though quite beautiful, she hides her good looks under the garb of mourning. A righteous woman, she fasts regularly and conducts herself beyond reproach.

Besides her physical attractiveness, she is also renowned for her wisdom. All people esteem her.

With Judith's city, Bethulia, under siege, food is scarce, and water is rationed. On day thirty-four, the mayor promises the people he'll surrender in five days, hoping God will miraculously save them before then. But Judith chastises him for giving in to the people's demands. She has a plan. It's a bold strategy to save them, but she won't tell anyone the details.

She cleans up and replaces her widow's clothing with festive attire, complete with perfume and jewelry. It's her most alluring look. The people can't believe her transformation. Then she and her trusted servant leave the city and allow themselves to be captured.

Promising to aid the enemy, her captors take Judith to their commander, Holofernes. Weaving partial truth into her ruse, Judith unveils her proposal of how she will advise him in taking the city with no loss of life. Enthralled by her beauty, Holofernes believes every word she says. Besides, he wants to sleep with her.

After a couple of days, and unwilling to wait any longer, he summons her to join him in his tent for dinner. They eat, and he drinks—too much. He sends everyone away so he can seduce her. He passes out instead, with Judith's virtue still intact. She grabs his sword, prays for supernatural strength, and decapitates him with two blows.

Judith and her servant sneak off before anyone knows what happened, carrying his severed head with them. Arriving home, the people celebrate as she tells them what happened and holds up the proof.

Achior sees the head of Holofernes and faints, falling on his face. Amazed at God's deliverance through Judith, Achior believes in God and is circumcised.

When the soldiers find the body of their headless leader, they're thrown into a panic and flee.

Wise Judith tells the people what to do, and they comply. The Jews in Bethulia summon their countrymen throughout Israel to give chase to the fleeing army, slaughtering their enemy and enjoying the spoils.

The people celebrate Judith for her heroic exploits. Judith dedicates her portion of the spoils to God. She grants freedom to her trusted servant. She lives to be 105 and is buried next to Manasseh. The people mourn her passing for seven days.

Taking much risk, Judith daringly delivers her people from their enemies, using her beauty to entice, while remaining pure.

Significant results require significant risk. How much are we willing to risk to do what God calls us to do? What can we do that no one else dares to do?

[Read about Judith in Judith 9–14 and Judith 16:1–17. Discover another wise and beautiful woman in 1 Samuel 25:3.]

GREEK ESTHER

Seeing the book of Esther listed in the Apocrypha may surprise you. That's because there are two versions of it.

The shorter one appears in the Old Testament and is the one most people know. The longer version in the Apocrypha expands the original. It's sometimes called Greek Esther, because the source manuscripts are in Greek and not Hebrew, as with the original version, which some call the Hebrew version of Esther.

As a writer, I appreciate these two variations. Sometimes, after writing a passage, I need to round out the text with additional details. This may occur quickly, but other times it happens much later. This is how I view Greek Esther—an appropriate expanded version of the original. (Other times when I finish writing a passage, I remove content to make it more concise and quicker to read. This might be a way to understand the Hebrew version.)

A concern of some is that the Hebrew version of Esther does not mention God. Yet the expanded version in Greek contains many mentions of him, providing a decided connection between God and the events of this story. In this way, the expanded version emerges as a more holistic understanding of God at work. It is, therefore, a more spiritually significant version.

All the verses of the original book of Esther appear in the expanded version, albeit sometimes revealing different details. Both versions contain the same chapter and verse designations that were later added to Scripture.

The expanded version of Esther also contains several additional passages. The added text appears interspersed throughout the book's ten chapters. Different translations of the Greek version of Esther use various means to note the additional passages, but most designate them with letters.

Here's an overview of the expanded sections, following the CEB translation.

Addition A: This precedes Esther 1:1 and serves as a helpful prologue and includes Mordecai's vision.

Addition B: Is inserted between Esther 3:13 and 14 and details Artaxerxes's first decree.

Addition C: Comes after Esther 4:17 and shares Mordecai and Esther's prayers for deliverance.

Addition D: Follows immediately after Addition C to expand Esther 5:1–2, giving insightful details.

Addition E: Falls between Esther 8:12 and 13. It's a copy of Artaxerxes's second decree.

Addition F: Appears after Esther 10:3 (the last verse in the original version) and serves as an epilogue. In it, Mordecai interprets the dream we read in the prologue (Addition A), which was fulfilled in the intervening chapters, serving as smart bookends for Greek Esther.

21: GABATHA AND THARRA

Gabatha and Tharra only appear once in Scripture. They are two eunuchs assigned to guard the courtyard. We can assume this is the courtyard of King Artaxerxes.

As Mordecai rests in the courtyard, he over-hears Gabatha and Tharra conspiring to attack the king.

Mordecai reports this to Artaxerxes, who confronts the pair. They confess, and he executes them. Artaxerxes notes Mordecai's actions in the official record and rewards him with gifts and a promotion.

For their part, Gabatha and Tharra could have denied Mordecai's claim. It would have been his word versus theirs. In fact, it would have been two against one.

But the pair chooses not to do this. They admit their wrongdoing, perhaps hoping for the king's mercy. But instead of receiving the mercy they desire, he gives them the judgment they deserve.

Fortunately for us today, through Jesus, God offers us mercy even though we deserve judgment.

Do we rely on God's mercy or fear his judgment? How can we rightly balance mercy with judgment?

[Read about Gabatha and Tharra in Greek Esther A:12–17 (the prologue to chapter 1). Discover more when King David opts for God's mercy in 2 Samuel 24:11–14.]

22: ARTAXERXES

rtaxerxes is king of the vast empire of the Persians and Medes. Besides the book of Esther, we also read about him in the books of Ezra, Nehemiah, and 1 & 2 Esdras.

After the prologue to Esther, the story opens with Artaxerxes giving a party. Most versions of the Bible call it a banquet or a feast, yet the CEB calls this six-month-long party a wedding feast, implicitly between Artaxerxes and Vashti. This detail gives us helpful context for what happens next.

After the six-month celebration, the king holds a six-day wine festival. He provides choice wine, and people can drink all they want. Queen Vashti holds her own six-day wine festival for the women of the palace.

On the seventh day, an inebriated King Artaxerxes orders Vashti to come before him and his guests. He wants to introduce her as queen and crown her.

Vashti refuses.

Artaxerxes is furious—and likely embarrassed. Raging with anger, he consults his advisors on what to do. One counselor tells him that Vashti has set a dangerous precedent, so he must give a decisive response. He should forever banish her from his presence and replace her with a more suitable queen.

Artaxerxes agrees.

How open are we to seek the advice of others? When have we followed someone's counsel when we shouldn't have?

[Read about Artaxerxes in Greek Esther 1:10–20 and Greek Esther 5:3–7. Discover another king who followed the advice of others in 1 Kings 12:1–14.]

23: VASHTI

When summoned to appear before King Artaxerxes and his guests, Vashti refuses.

But we don't know why.

One thought is that she's also inebriated from her own wine festival and not thinking clearly. Or perhaps she doesn't want to debase herself before the ogling eyes of a bunch of drunken men. A third consideration is that she seeks to establish early in their marriage that she will not do what her husband tells her to do if she doesn't want to do it.

It's this third consideration that's most likely, given the discussion that follows. And if this isn't the queen's motivation, the king's advisors assume it is.

Regardless, they worry her example will embolden all wives throughout the realm to disobey and disrespect their husbands.

Memucan voices this concern. He recommends a permanent banning of Vashti from the king's presence and finding a more suitable—that is, a more obedient—replacement. Once communicated throughout the kingdom, it will establish fear and respect in every home.

Note that just because the Bible reports this as Memucan's recommendation, we'd be wrong to assume this is God's perspective. It is not. Throughout Scripture, God seeks to elevate women, whereas sinful men try to push them down. Such is the case in this story.

For her part, Vashti suffers because of her stand. The king banishes her from his presence and strips her of her title. In effect, he divorces her most publicly. Given this, it's easy to imagine everyone else ostracizing her, fearing their own well-being if they associate with her.

What risks are we willing to take to do what's right? How willing are we to stand with those society views as outcasts?

[Read about Vashti in Greek Esther 1:9–20. Discover another person who refused to obey a king in Daniel 6:5–15.]

24: MEMUCAN

Memucan only appears in one story in Scripture. It's when he gives advice to King Artaxerxes about Queen Vashti's refusal to obey him.

Memucan speaks when all the king's other advisors do not. Perhaps he voices his opinion first, which ends further discussion. Or it may be no one knows what to do, while he has an idea.

Regardless, Memucan gives his advice and no one else does. The king likes what Memucan says—and so does everyone else. We're left wondering if they really agree with him or are reluctant to offer a conflicting perspective.

When faced with a predicament, do we agree with the first idea we hear? How willing are we to consider multiple perspectives before we decide what to do?

[Read about Memucan in Greek Esther 1:16–22. Discover another instance of giving a king advice in 2 Samuel 17:1–14.]

25: HAMAN

Haman is a wealthy man and an esteemed advisor to King Artaxerxes. At one point, he's the second in command. He's also the nemesis of Mordecai, Esther's cousin and guardian. We first encounter Haman in the prologue to Esther, which reveals insight into his motivation.

When Mordecai hears Gabatha and Tharra conspire to attack the king, Mordecai reports them, and the king executes them. Their death begins Haman's vendetta against Mordecai. Haman wants to make Mordecai pay for what he did to bring about Gabatha and Tharra's death.

Haman's desire for vengeance further escalates when Mordecai refuses to bow before him, as decreed by the king. But Haman is no longer satisfied with merely killing Mordecai. Instead, he now schemes to kill all Jews because of what Mordecai did.

He almost succeeds, too, except that Artaxerxes's new queen is also Jewish and takes bold action to save her people.

When have we let vengeance cause us to do wrong? Is taking revenge ever justified?

[Read about Haman in Greek Esther A:17 and Greek Esther 3:1–6. Discover another story of disproportionate revenge in Genesis 34:25–29.]

26: MORDECAI (1)

Mordecai is a Jew, exiled when Nebuchadnezzar conquers the nation of Judah. He also cares for his cousin Esther after her parents die.

Mordecai earns the ire of Haman for his role in bringing about the execution of Gabatha and Tharra. Compounding this, Mordecai refuses to bow before Haman as the king decreed. This isn't a matter of pride but of principle, for he refuses to honor anyone above God, his Lord.

Because Mordecai is Jewish, Haman wants to kill all Jews and not just Mordecai. He may reason that if Jewish Mordecai won't bow before him, no other Jews will either. Therefore, they must all die. With Artaxerxes's tacit approval, Haman issues a decree for the annihilation of all Jews across the realm.

Mordecai is distraught when he learns that his personal stand to not bow before Haman has put the lives of all Jews at risk. Yet, he affirms his decision to not honor any person above God as being the right choice.

With Esther now living in the palace, Mordecai encourages her to act on their people's behalf to save them from extermination.

Along with the Jewish people, Mordecai and Esther fast and pray for deliverance.

When has a personal decision we made negatively affected others? When have we sought God for deliverance?

[Read about Mordecai in Greek Esther 2:5–23, Greek Esther 3:1–7, and Greek Esther C:1–10. Discover another time people fasted for deliverance in Jonah 3:4–10.]

27: ZERESH

Zeresh is the wife of Haman. One day he leaves the king's court elated, but Mordecai's presence at the gate—presumably refusing to bow before him—deflates him.

Haman goes home and vents. He brags about his wealth, position, and honor. But these give him no joy because of Mordecai the Jew.

In response, Zeresh (along with his friends' accord) suggests he erect a pole seventy-five feet high and request the king's permission to impale Mordecai on it. This idea pleases Haman, and he has the pole prepared.

The next day he rises early to seek Artaxerxes's approval, yet he unexpectedly ends up being commanded to honor Mordecai instead. Mortified, he complies and returns home humiliated.

When he tells Zeresh and his friends what happened, they predict Haman's fall because Mordecai has the living God with him.

Zeresh tells Haman what he wanted to hear about executing Mordecai. What if she had advised him differently?

Do we tell people what they want to hear or speak truth? How can we better encourage our family and friends to do what is right?

[Read about Zeresh in Greek Esther 5:9–14 and Greek Esther 6:13. Discover another wife who gave poor advice to her husband in Genesis 3:6.]

28: HEGAI

When King Artaxerxes's advisors recommend finding a replacement for Queen Vashti, they gather many beautiful virgins for the king to try out. Yes, it's as bad as it sounds.

Esther, Mordecai's cousin, is one girl selected. She, along with all the other girls, enters the "women's house" under the care of the eunuch Hegai. He supplies them with beauty treatments for twelve months. Then they await their turn to go to the king.

Esther wins Hegai's favor, and he gives her special consideration. This includes select foods and seven servants to attend to her.

When it's Esther's turn to go to the king, Hegai advises her, and she follows his recommendations.

She wins the king's favor.

Do we give good advice to others? How well do we do at following the advice given to us?

[Read about Hegai in Greek Esther 2:8–15. Discover the advice given to Absalom and see who he listens to in 2 Samuel 17:1–14.]

29: SHAASHGAZ

Shaashgaz, like Hegai, is also a eunuch who oversees a group of women.

After a woman leaves Hegai's care to see the king, she then transfers to Shaashgaz's group of "secondary wives." They are the women the king didn't select. He rejected them. Though he can request to see them again, we wonder how often he does.

In overseeing the house of virgins, as they await their time to be with the king, Hegai spends his time with girls excited about their future. They hope the king will select them and crown them queen. We can imagine it's a mostly positive environment.

Shaashgaz, however, oversees the house filled with women the king doesn't want. Their future is bleak. They have little to look forward to. We can suspect it's a mostly negative environment. And it's Shaashgaz's lot to oversee it.

How do we react when we receive a less-than-ideal assignment? What can we do to make the best of a trying situation?

[Read about Shaashgaz in Greek Esther 2:14. Discover another man who found himself in a trying situation—and see what happens—in Genesis 39:20–23.]

30: ESTHER

Esther, the cousin of Mordecai, is a beautiful young woman. She's one of the many girls selected as a possible replacement for Queen Vashti. When it's her turn to spend the night with the king, she pleases him. He marries her and makes her the new queen. Throughout this, she keeps her ethnicity a secret, as Mordecai instructed.

When Queen Esther hears about the edict to annihilate the Jews throughout the kingdom, she prays and fasts. In her heartfelt plea, she confesses she detests sleeping with the king, as an uncircumcised foreigner. She hates her crown, only wearing it when she must appear in public. Hers is not a happily-ever-after Cinderella story but more so one of abhorrent obligation.

When she goes, unsummoned, before the king to plead for her people's lives, he doesn't raise his scepter to recognize her, and she faints in fear. With compassion, he leaps up to comfort her and assure her she won't die—that rule only applies to "ordinary people," he says.

She requests he and Haman come to a special dinner. Then she invites them back a second night and she then reveals Haman's plot to kill the Jews—which includes her.

King Artaxerxes orders Haman's execution on the pole he intended for Mordecai. The king gives Esther Haman's estate and empowers Mordecai to issue a counter-edict to offset the one from Haman. Out of fear, many Gentiles convert and are circumcised.

Because of the new edict, the Jews avoid being killed and instead kill many of their enemies.

To commemorate these events, Mordecai institutes the celebration of the Purim, colloquially known as Mordecai's day (2 Maccabees 15:36).

And none of this would have happened had Esther not been in her royal position and risked her life to intercede for her people.

If we're not in the position we want to be, do we complain or use it to accomplish God's will? How do we react when we find ourselves in a situation that goes against what we believe?

[Read about Esther in Greek Esther 2:7–18, Greek Esther C:12–30, and Greek Esther D:1–15. Discover another woman who rescues her people in Judges 4:4–16.]

31: TEN SONS OF HAMAN

Haman is dead, but his ten sons live on. They can continue his line. Their names are Parshandatha, Dalphon, Aspatha, Poratha, Adalia, Aridatha, Parmashta, Arisai, Aridai, and Vaizatha.

Yet when the Jews follow Mordecai's edict that allows them to defend themselves against their enemies, they kill Haman's ten sons too. What we don't know is if they are true enemies of the Jews—just like their father—or if they were innocent of his hateful vendetta and killed merely because they were Haman's sons.

It's possible Haman passed his hatred for the Jews to his boys, and that they would have tried to finish what he could not.

But it's also possible that Haman's sons saw the error of their father (or repented from following it) but were judged guilty merely because of their relation to him.

What have we learned from our parents that we need to not follow? What can we do to make sure we don't pass negative attitudes to our family?

[Read about the ten sons of Haman in Greek Esther 9:7–14. Discover other people killed for what their ancestor did in 2 Samuel 21:1–9.]

32: DOSITHEUS (2)

Dositheus is a priest who shows up only in the epilogue of Greek Esther. Though he may be a contemporary of Mordecai, he more likely comes along later.

Regardless, Dositheus affirms he's a priest, likely able to produce his genealogical records to confirm it. He and his son, Ptolemy (2), take Mordecai's letter about the Purim and authenticate it.

Then his grandson, Lysimachus, who lives in Jerusalem, translates it. We can assume he translates it into Hebrew, but Greek is another consideration.

Since Dositheus is a priest, his son and grandson would be part of the priestly line too. In safeguarding Mordecai's letter, Dositheus, Ptolemy, and Lysimachus all work to preserve it for future generations.

Though Dositheus couldn't do this all himself, he raised a son and grandson who shared his vision to save this piece of history. And Lysimachus completed what his grandfather began by translating it so more people could read it.

What legacy are we passing to future generations? What can we do to preserve Scripture for others to read?

[Read about Dositheus in Greek Esther F:11. Discover another man who preserved Scripture for future generations in Daniel 12:4.]

WISDOM

Wisdom—sometimes called the Wisdom of Solomon—is reminiscent of the book of Proverbs, which is mostly penned by Solomon.

Both books contain sage advice that can guide us into right living. While Proverbs contains concise snippets of actionable applications, Wisdom is more thought-provoking and insightful, although just as actionable. It also references several Old Testament accounts.

We attribute Wisdom to Solomon. But the text doesn't confirm this. Maybe Solomon did indeed write it, or perhaps an unknown scribe compiled the book in his honor. Regardless, the identity of the author shouldn't distract us from the truth its words contain.

Just as with Proverbs, the name Wisdom (as in Proverbs 1:20, Proverbs 8:11–12, and Proverbs 9:1) again appears in Wisdom, personified as *she*. See Wisdom 6:12, Wisdom 6:22, Wisdom 7:24, and many more verses.

The book of Wisdom has much to teach us if only we will listen.

33: SOLOMON

Aside from some first-person passages, primarily in Wisdom chapters 7 and 8, the book of Wisdom gives us no direct information about Solomon and his life. But the rest of Scripture does. He appears in eleven Old Testament books, six books of the Apocrypha, and four New Testament books.

Here are the key points:

Solomon is the third king of Israel and the son of King David.

God appears to Solomon (something he rarely does in the Old Testament) and pledges to give the king whatever he wishes. Solomon asks for wisdom and knowledge to lead well. God grants the king the wisdom and knowledge he requested and also gives him wealth, riches, and fame, which he could have asked for but didn't (2 Chronicles 1:7–12).

The Bible declares Solomon as the wisest of men (1 Kings 4:29–34), and the queen of Sheba confirms it (1 Kings 10:6–8).

Despite all his wisdom, Solomon makes some foolish mistakes too. Chief is that he lets his foreign wives distract him from solely worshiping God. As a result, God pledges to tear the kingdom from him (1 Kings 11:7–13 and Nehemiah 13:26).

Solomon started well, but he didn't finish strong. And how we wrap up our life matters most.

Though we shouldn't view God as a genie that grants wishes, if God asked what we desired, what would we request? Regardless of how our lives start, what must we do to finish strong?

[Read about Solomon in Wisdom 7:1–14. Read about Wisdom in Wisdom 9:9–11. Discover other men who married foreign wives in Ezra 10:1–14 and again in Nehemiah 13:23–31.]

SIRACH

The book of Sirach, also called Ecclesiasticus (not to be confused with Ecclesiastes), is another piece of wisdom literature. It's a compilation of sayings, presented in style and content like Proverbs. As such, it's a valuable collection of practical advice and wise sayings.

It's also the longest book in the Apocrypha.

Sirach uses some delightful descriptive names for God. Besides the common *Lord*, we have *Lord Almighty* (Sirach 42:17), *Father* (Sirach 23:1, 4), *the one* (Sirach 18:1 and many more), and *the Most High* (such as in Sirach 12:2).

The concluding chapters of Sirach (44 through

50) pay tribute to notable figures in Hebrew history, providing us with valuable insights into each one. It reads like a celebration of prominent Old Testament characters.

They are Enoch, Noah, Abraham, Isaac, Jacob, Moses, Aaron, Phinehas, Joshua, Caleb, Samuel, Nathan, David, Solomon, Elijah, Elisha, Hezekiah, Isaiah, Josiah, Ezekiel, Zerubbabel, Joshua, and Nehemiah, with brief mentions of Joseph, Shem, Seth, and Adam.

Some translations of the Apocrypha alternately call it "The Wisdom of Jesus the Son of Sirach." The CEB, however—which we're using as our basis for study—simply calls it Sirach.

Aside from the previously mentioned Old Testament characters, the book of Sirach only introduces a few more people: Simon and two men named Jesus.

34: SIMON (11)

Simon is a high priest, the son of Onias. Sirach calls him a *great* high priest.

He repairs the temple and strengthens its defenses, fortifying its structure. He also creates a reservoir as large as a lake. And he works to keep the people safe from disaster and secure from sieges.

The people adore him. And he exhorts them to bless God, seek him for peace, and receive his mercy.

Though we know little about Simon, we see how he affects the people to facilitate their worship and provide for their safety.

What can we do to help people better worship God? How might we exhort those we influence?

[Read about Simon in Sirach 50:1–4. Discover another temple repair in Ezra 6:13–18.]

35: JESUS (4)

Jesus (1), our Lord and Savior, is the star of the New Testament and the central figure in our faith—even in all of history. Yet his name is not unique in Scripture. We see Jesus (2), also known as Justus, in Colossians.

There are two more men named Jesus. Both are in the book of Sirach. In considering them, realize that the match of names is not significant and nothing more than a coincidence.

Jesus (3) is the grandfather of Sirach (verse 7 of the prologue).

Jesus (4) is the son of Sirach (Sirach 50:27). He is the scribe who compiled the book or, alternatively, who translated it.

As the book of Sirach wraps up, Jesus (4)

records his prayer for us to read. It stands as both an example and an encouragement. He gives thanks to God and praises him, acknowledging him as protector and helper, who answers prayer and rescues.

How can our prayers be an example to others? Should we spend more time thanking God and praising him?

[Read about Jesus (4) in Sirach 50:27 and Sirach 51:1–12. Discover another important scribe in Jeremiah 36:4–32.]

BARUCH

Baruch is a disciple, follower, and trusted friend of Jeremiah. He's also the scribe who records Jeremiah's words as he dictates them (Jeremiah 36:4). They both live in Judah when the book of Jeremiah is written, but they won't remain there for long.

It's this Baruch, the scribe of Jeremiah, who writes the book of Baruch. It serves as a fitting follow-up to the book of Jeremiah, since it's written after the people's exile to Babylon.

After the introduction, Baruch contains a confession of the nation of Israel's guilt and prayer for deliverance, much like Daniel's prayer in Daniel 9. A section of poetry follows this.

Some versions of the Apocrypha add a sixth chapter to the book of Baruch, which shares the letter of Jeremiah. The CEB, however, wisely keeps Jeremiah's epistle as a separate one-chapter book, which follows the book of Baruch.

36: BARUCH (1)

Baruch, Jeremiah's faithful scribe and assistant, is the son of Neriah, the son of Mahseiah. Most of what we know about Baruch appears in the book of Jeremiah, a document that Baruch recorded most, if not all, of at Jeremiah's behest.

Besides serving as Jeremiah's scribe, Baruch also speaks for the prophet when he cannot because Jeremiah's in hiding or in prison.

This earns Baruch the ire of Jeremiah's detractors. As a result, the faithful scribe also suffers for doing God's work.

The last time we read of Baruch in the book of Jeremiah is Jeremiah's prophetic words about his scribe. Imagine taking dictation for a man of God and then writing what the Almighty says about *you*. This brief instruction from God, through Jeremiah, to Baruch ends with the Lord's promise that wherever Baruch goes, God will let him escape with his life.

In the book of Jeremiah, we learn that when the people flee to Egypt to avoid King Nebuchadnezzar's assaults, they drag Jeremiah and Baruch with them. But Baruch later resurfaces in Babylon and prophesies to God's people there. In this, we see the fulfillment of Jeremiah's prophecy for his scribe.

If we're faithful to God, will he always rescue us? When we're persecuted for obeying God, do we give up or persevere?

[Read about Baruch in Baruch 1:1, 3, and 8. Discover more in Jeremiah 32:12–16, Jeremiah 36:4–32, Jeremiah 43:1–7, and Jeremiah 45:1–5.]

37: JECONIAH

Jeconiah is king of Judah during its last days as a nation. He's the son of King Jehoiakim, the son of King Josiah, as well as a descendant of King Solomon and part of King David's royal line.

King Nebuchadnezzar takes Jeconiah prisoner and deports him to Babylon.

What we read about him in the Bible often uses his exile as a marker to establish the time when other events occur (such as in Jeremiah and Esther).

In the book of Baruch, Jeconiah is present when Baruch reads the words of the scroll. This is after Nebuchadnezzar razes the temple in Jerusalem. It is a dark time for God's people.

As the former king, Jeconiah

no doubt wonders how his actions contributed to Judah being conquered and their exile to Babylon. Could he have done anything different? Does he feel remorse for not being a better king? What does he regret?

From his bleak existence, he surely wonders about his future and the future of his people. Though Jeremiah prophesies restoration, will Jeconiah

live to see it?

What changes should we make now so we don't have regrets later? When our situation is bleak, how well do we trust God with our future?

[Read about Jeconiah in Baruch 1:3 and Baruch 1:9. Discover more in Jeremiah 28:4.]

38: BELSHAZZAR

We mostly know about Belshazzar from the book of Daniel (Daniel 5).

From Daniel, we know Belshazzar succeeds his father Nebuchadnezzar as ruler over Babylon. Once established, he throws a grand party for one thousand of his nobles. While drinking wine, he orders that the goblets taken from the temple in Jerusalem be brought out to serve his guests. In doing so, they praise their gods.

Suddenly, disembodied fingers appear and write four words on the wall. The sight shakes Belshazzar to his core. His face turns pale, and his knees weaken.

To his dismay, no one can read the words or

decipher their meaning. At the suggestion of the queen, he calls for Daniel to interpret the message.

Daniel reads the words and explains what they mean: "Your days are numbered. Yes, your days are numbered. You've been judged and fall short. Your kingdom will be taken from you and given to the Medes and Persians."

Despite knowing what happened to Nebuchadnezzar when pride overtook him, Belshazzar repeated his father's error. He refused to humble himself. That night, Darius the Mede seizes the kingdom and kills Belshazzar, just as Daniel predicted.

But before this happens, Baruch reads his scroll to the people. He mentions Belshazzar twice.

First, there is the admonition to pray for the lives of Nebuchadnezzar and Belshazzar, that their time here on earth will be like heaven.

Next, he acknowledges that the people live under Nebuchadnezzar's and Belshazzar's protection, serving them for a long time and finding favor.

These two passages seem like an extreme perspective to have for the rulers who conquered their nation, killed many of their friends and relatives, and sent them into exile.

Given that Babylon is later conquered, and

Belshazzar is killed, we're left to wonder how many people prayed for him and truly meant what they requested.

How well do we do at praying for our leaders? If we don't like them, or if they oppose God's ways, should we pray for them anyway?

[Read about Belshazzar in Baruch 1:11–12. Discover more about praying for our leaders in 1 Timothy 2:2.]

LETTER OF JEREMIAH

The Letter of Jeremiah, or the Epistle of Jeremiah, is a note of encouragement written by Jeremiah and sent to the exiles living in Babylon. (He is likely in Egypt at this time.) The theme of the letter encourages the Jews in Babylon to avoid idols and idol worship, something that brought about the downfall of Judah at the hands of Nebuchadnezzar.

A short one-chapter book, the Letter of Jeremiah is comparable to Jeremiah's letter recorded in Jeremiah 29:1–23. We also see similar language in Jeremiah 10:2–28.

Some versions of the Apocrypha—although not the CEB—include the Letter of Jeremiah as an addendum to the book of Baruch, making it Baruch 6.

Though Baruch did not write the letter, he may have preserved it and added it to his other writings. This is understandable, since Baruch was the scribe who helped Jeremiah record the prophet's writings for the book of Jeremiah.

Though the fleeing people haul Jeremiah off to Egypt along with Baruch, the next time we see Baruch, he's in Babylon. We don't know how he gets there, but he likely carried Jeremiah's letter with him.

39: JEREMIAH

J eremiah, the son of Hilkiah, is both a prophet and a priest. The book of Jeremiah covers his life and ministry, but Baruch compiles the content based on Jeremiah's dictation and adds details about the prophet's life. Because of this, we know more about Jeremiah than any of the other prophets in the Bible.

Through the book of Jeremiah, we see how he suffers for speaking God's word to an unreceptive audience. At various times, his detractors threaten him, throw him into a pit, and place him in stocks. More than once, his life is in danger. False prophets oppose him. They humiliate him. And though he tells the people not to flee to Egypt, they do exactly that and drag him with them.

One thing unique to Jeremiah's prophecy is that —unlike other prophets—he gives a specific timeline to one of his pronouncements. He says the people will live in exile in Babylon for seventy years (Jeremiah 25:11–12).

Four chapters later, he adds more detail. Jeremiah says that after the seventy years of captivity have passed, God will rescue them and bring them home (Jeremiah 29:10). He will also punish the king of Babylon (Jeremiah 50:18).

In the Letter of Jeremiah, we see the faithful prophet continuing to minister to the people. His commitment to continue to serve the people who ignored and persecuted him provides us with an example to persevere in what God calls us to do.

How do we react when we encounter opposition for obeying God? Should we be concerned if we never face persecution for how we live our lives?

[Read about Jeremiah in the introduction to the Letter of Jeremiah. Discover more about this prophet in Jeremiah 43:1–7, 2 Chronicles 36:21–23, and Daniel 9:2.]

PRAYER OF AZARIAH

The Prayer of Azariah also goes by Song of the Three Young Men or The Song of the Three Holy Children in other versions of the Apocrypha, yet Prayer of Azariah seems like the best title to me.

In this one-chapter book, Hananiah, Mishael, and Azariah (whom we may better know as Shadrach, Meshach, and Abednego) refuse to bow to the king's statue. As punishment, Nebuchadnezzar orders them thrown into an inferno to burn them alive. We read the account in Daniel 3.

The intent is their execution, but God protects

them. Much to the king's astonishment, they walk around in the furnace, unharmed.

While in the inferno, they sing and pray. This book records their words. In it we read Azariah's confident prayer, followed by a bold refrain from all three.

Amazed, the king calls them to come out of the furnace, and then he too affirms God.

Though the CEB gives the Prayer of Azariah its spotlight as a separate book, many versions of the Apocrypha integrate it into Daniel 3 by inserting the text between verses 23 and 24. This provides a more comprehensive reading within the context of the story.

40: AZARIAH (23)

One of the three men Nebuchadnezzar throws into the inferno for refusing to worship the golden statue is Azariah. Azariah is his Jewish name, but we may better know him by Abednego, the Babylonian name assigned to him.

Though the book of Daniel mostly calls him Abednego, the Prayer of Azariah only uses Abednego once, instead honoring him with his given Jewish name of Azariah.

In Scripture, when Azariah (or alternately Abednego) appears as part of a trio, his name always occurs last. We don't know why, but it does. Is he the youngest? The least esteemed? The one most often overlooked?

With one lone exception, we always read of him with his two friends. And that one time is his bold prayer as the flames of the furnace surround him and his two buddies. Yet Azariah is the one to speak first. He prays. His two friends listen.

His prayer isn't a desperate plea for help.

Instead, he begins by praising God and then confessing the people's past sin and God's just response. It's not until near the end that he even asks God to rescue them. But even this isn't for the sake of him and his friends, but more so that God will receive honor above all.

How should we react when our name appears last? When we face trouble, do we focus on our problem or how the situation could honor God?

[Read about Azariah in the Prayer of Azariah 1:1–22. Discover more about worshiping in Exodus 20:1–7.]

41: HANANIAH, MISHAEL, AND AZARIAH

Whenen Babylon conquers Judah, Daniel and his three friends are seized and deported. The three friends are Hananiah, Mishael, and Azariah, but the book of Daniel usually calls this trio by the names their Babylonian captors give them: Shadrach, Meshach, and Abednego.

The Prayer of Azariah, however, uses their Jewish names of Hananiah, Mishael, and Azariah. With one exception (as covered in the preceding chapter) they always appear as a trio. Therefore, we'll consider them as a unit, a team. Recall that it's hard to snap a three-ply cord (Ecclesiastes 4:12).

So it is with Hananiah, Mishael, and Azariah. Together, they are strong.

They refuse to bow to the golden statue, as King Nebuchadnezzar decreed. Instead, they pledge to stay true to God, who can save them from the king's fiery furnace of death. But even if he doesn't, they'll still worship him alone.

Nebuchadnezzar orders to burn them alive.

This is when Azariah voices his confident, God-honoring prayer. Emboldened, his two friends join him when he finishes. The three sing hymns of praise and blessing to God. Though still in the furnace, they wrap up their song by thanking God for his rescue from certain death.

Though surrounded by flames, the fire doesn't consume them. The king calls them to come forth, and they emerge unaffected by the inferno. Amazed, Nebuchadnezzar praises God, even though he doesn't know who God is. The king decrees that anyone who says a word against their God must die.

How willing are we to suffer and even die for our faith? Do we go through life on our own or with others as a "three-ply cord"?

[Read about Hananiah, Mishael, and Azariah in Prayer of Azariah 1:28–67. Discover more in Isaiah 43:2 and Daniel 3.]

SUSANNA

The book of Susanna focuses on the pious life and crooked trial of the righteous Susanna. Falsely accused of adultery, she's sentenced to die. A young Daniel plays a pivotal role in the outcome.

This is a story of steadfast faith, of doing what is right regardless of the cost, and of the power of Holy Spirit insight.

In the CEB, Susanna is a one-chapter tale of valor, but in some versions of the Apocrypha, it's added to the end of Daniel as a thirteenth chapter.

42: JOAKIM (1)

J oakim lives in Babylon. He is the husband of Susanna. And he is rich—not a little rich, but a lot, as in *very* rich.

Don't rush past this. Most likely, Nebuchadnezzar exiles Joakim to Babylon when he conquers the nation of Judah. We can suspect Joakim had to leave his wealth behind. So, if he was wealthy in Judah, his wealth stayed there.

How does he become wealthy in Babylon? He may have obeyed what the prophet Jeremiah tells the people to do.

Jeremiah sends a letter to the exiled nation. In that message, he tells them to settle down in Babylon, to build houses and grow gardens, to get married and increase in number (Jeremiah 29:4–6).

In short, they should seek to prosper in this foreign land they were forced to inhabit.

Apparently, Joakim does just that. As a result, he becomes *very* wealthy. God blesses him.

He owns a large, private garden, stationed next to his home. It serves as a gathering place for the Jews in the area because the people hold him in such high esteem.

Two elders are appointed to serve as judges that year, and they hold court at Joakim's place. His home is the place to be, which establishes the scene for the story of Susanna.

What should our view of wealth be? Whether we have much or little, how can we best serve God with it?

[Read about Joakim in Susanna 1:1–6. Discover another blessed man in Genesis 18:18 and Genesis 24:1.]

43: TWO ELDERS

Though the book of Susanna is about her, most of the story addresses two unnamed elders. Appointed as judges for the year, they are corrupt.

These two elders don't care about God or about justice. Instead, they focus on their desires. They see the beautiful Susanna and lust for her. At first, each one keeps his shameful desires to himself. But one day they admit to each other their longing to have sex with her. They plan how to make it happen.

They hide in her garden while everyone else leaves for lunch.

Wishing to bathe, Susanna locks the gate and sends her servants into the house to fetch supplies. The two elders reveal themselves and solicit her.

They say that if she declines, they'll tell everyone they saw her cheating on her husband with a young man.

Susanna refuses, and the two elders do exactly as threatened. The next day they testify they caught Susanna in the act of adultery. They claim they tried to restrain the man, but he got away, and Susanna wouldn't say who he was.

The people believe the lying judges and sentence the innocent Susanna to die.

When have we used our position to do something we shouldn't have? What can we do to make sure we care about God and justice?

[Read about the two elders in Susanna 1:5–41. Discover two other corrupt leaders in 1 Samuel 2:22–25.]

44: SUSANNA

Susanna is an extremely beautiful woman and honored by God. She is the wife of esteemed Joakim and the daughter of Hilkiah.

One day, after everyone leaves for lunch, she wants to bathe in the garden to cool off. It's a hot day. She locks the gate to the garden. She sends her two servants inside to get some olive oil and lotion. That's when two men come out from hiding. It's the two elders. They both want to have sex with her. They threaten her if she won't.

She's in a no-win situation. If she refuses, they'll accuse her of adultery and condemn her to death. Yet if she submits, she'll be guilty of adultery before the Lord. She prefers a clear conscience before God, so she tells them no and screams for help.

The two elders scream too. One opens the gate. Her family and servants come running to see what all the commotion is about.

The elders claim they caught her with a man, but he got away.

A day later, the pair give false testimony against Susanna. The people believe the lying judges and sentence Susanna to die.

Her worst fears are about to happen. She will soon die for something she didn't do. They lead her to her execution.

How do we respond when confronted with a no-win situation? Do we believe God will vindicate us when accused of something we didn't do?

[Read about Susanna in Susanna 1:22–63. Discover a similar situation in Genesis 39:6-18.]

45: DANIEL

After being falsely condemned to death, Susanna screams as they lead her away to her execution. She proclaims her innocence and begs God to save her.

God hears her plea, and the Holy Spirit gives insight to a young man named Daniel. He shouts, "I'm innocent of her death!"

This gets the people's attention.

Daniel chastises them for not questioning Susanna about what happened. Even though no one asked her side of the story, they now know. But it's her word against theirs—her against two respected elders and judges.

How can they discover the truth? Daniel proposes a wise solution.

He tells them to sequester one elder while he questions the other. His wise and discerning question is simple: "What kind of tree was the couple under when you saw them?"

The elder says, "A clove tree."

When Daniel asks the other elder the same question, he replies, "Under a yew."

In doing so, Daniel exposes their testimonies as lies. This vindicates Susanna.

Daniel also supernaturally receives insight about each elder.

To the first, he says, "Your sins have caught up with you. You have judged unfairly, punishing the innocent and freeing the guilty."

To the second elder, Daniel has an even more stinging rebuke. "You're a heathen and seduced by beauty. Your unrestrained sexual desire has warped your thinking. Though many women have given in to your demands in the past, Susanna would not."

With Susanna acquitted, the two discredited elders receive the punishment they tried to inflict on her.

By listening to the Holy Spirit and acting upon it, Daniel discovers the truth. Susanna goes free and her accusers die.

How well do we do at listening for Holy Spirit insight? How well do we do at following through?

[Read about Daniel in Susanna 1:45–61. We'll also read part 2 of Daniel's story in the section on Bel and the Dragon. Discover another wise decision to uncover the truth in 1 Kings 3:16–28.]

46: HILKIAH (14)

Hilkiah is the father of Susanna. He and his wife show up as incidental characters in the story of Susanna. Even so, we learn three things about them.

First, they are present at Susanna's trial, along with her children (their grandchildren) and other relatives. In doing so, Hilkiah and his wife show their support for their daughter during one of the darkest moments of her life.

Next, Hilkiah and his wife celebrate their daughter's acquittal. They give thanks to God, who heard her cry for help and rescued her through Daniel's wise cross-examination.

Last, we can implicitly credit them with raising a God-honoring and chaste daughter who did the right thing when confronted with a life-threatening dilemma.

Who can we stand with during their dark times of life? How can we better thank God for his work in our lives?

[Read about Hilkiah in Susanna 1:63. Discover another parent who stood by her son during his darkest hour in John 19:25.]

BEL AND THE DRAGON

Bel and the Dragon take place later in Daniel's life. This one-chapter book has two stories. Think of them as Daniel versus Bel and Daniel versus the Dragon. These two events then tie together to bring about a powerful climax.

Daniel has risen to a position of power and gained many enemies because of his faith and his success.

One day, King Cyrus confronts Daniel to discuss his beliefs.

First, the king insists Bel is a living god, but Daniel disagrees, asserting that Bel is nothing more than an inert idol. The king proposes a test to see who is right. The outcome has life-and-death rami-fications for Daniel.

Then Cyrus shifts his attention to a dragon the people worship as a living god. Daniel also dismisses the dragon as a god.

As a result, Daniel's enemies pressure the king to throw Daniel into a pit of lions. He stays there for six days.

Bel and the Dragon is a delightful tale of placing our trust in God. The CEB makes this one-chapter story its own book, but some versions of the Apocrypha tack this story to the end of Daniel as a fourteenth chapter, following the thirteenth chapter about Susanna.

[Some versions of the CEB call this book "Bel and the Snake," but "Bel and the Dragon" is the more common name.]

47: CYRUS

C yrus is the king of Persia during the life of Daniel. Throughout his time in Babylon, Daniel serves under several kings, with Cyrus being the last. At this time, Daniel is quite old, possibly in his seventies or eighties.

Most of the mentions of King Cyrus in Scripture appear simply to establish a time frame for the surrounding text. A notable exception is when the king allows the displaced peoples of Judah the opportunity to return to their homeland. Another exception is here in Bel and the Dragon.

The text notes that Daniel is a companion of King Cyrus, as well as an honored advisor. Within that context, it's simple to imagine a playful banter unfolding between Cyrus and Daniel.

As we read through Bel and the Dragon, this easygoing exchange flows freely between them, albeit amid some intense drama and a few inflammatory outbursts by the king.

The pair's close relationship serves as an anchor for this book's stories.

Who are we a companion to? Who is our companion?

[Read about Cyrus in Bel and the Dragon 1:1–4. Discover more about Cyrus in 2 Chronicles 36:22–23, Ezra 1:1–11, and Isaiah 45:1–8.]

48: BEL

As an idol, Bel is not a person but an inanimate object that the people revere.

King Cyrus—along with the Babylonians—worships Bel. Daniel does not. He worships God.

The Letter of Jeremiah, which decries idol worship, even mocks Bel (Letter of Jeremiah 1:40–41). This letter has been in Babylon for many years. It's possible Daniel is familiar with it or has even read it.

The king asks Daniel why he doesn't worship Bel.

Daniel laughs. "I don't honor manmade idols, but only the living God."

The king claims Bel is alive, too, as evidenced by

all the food he eats. Each night they leave food for him and each morning it's gone.

But Daniel insists Bel isn't eating it. He can't.

The king proposes a test and Daniel agrees. But if he's wrong, he'll be executed.

That night, Bel's priests bring his food to the temple as usual. As the priests wait outside, the king and Daniel set out the food and drink inside the temple, sealing the doors when they leave. But, unbeknownst to the priests, Daniel first has his servants sprinkle a dusting of ash over the temple floor.

The next morning, the seal remains unbroken. Cyrus and Daniel look inside. The food is gone! But Daniel directs the king's attention to the floor, which shows the footprints of many men, women, and children.

They entered the sealed temple through a secret passage and ate the food, just as they did every night.

The king has all the priests and their families killed. He turns Bel and the temple over to Daniel. Daniel destroys the idol and razes the temple.

Bel is no more.

Daniel risks his life to reveal the truth. How willing are we to do the same? What things serve as our modern-day idols?

[Read about Bel in Bel and the Dragon 1:3–22. Discover more about Bel in Isaiah 46:1, Jeremiah 50:2, and Jeremiah 51:44.]

49: THE DRAGON

The dragon is the second—and last—nonhuman we'll cover in this book. The people of Babylon also worship the dragon as a god. Don't think of this as a mythical dragon but an actual animal. (I envision a Komodo dragon.)

Though Cyrus failed to show that Bel was alive, it's obvious that the dragon is. And because it's living, Cyrus expects Daniel to worship it as a living god instead of *the* living God.

Again, Daniel declines, pledging to worship his Lord and God.

To prove the dragon has no power, Daniel says he can kill it without using a sword or a stick.

The king agrees, granting Daniel permission.

Daniel mixes a concoction of tar, grease, and hair. He feeds it to the dragon. The dragon swallows it and bursts open. The dragon is dead.

"That," Daniel says, "is what you've been worshiping."

Though we don't worship animals today, what might we worship instead of God? How willing are we to stand up to authority to combat false worship?

[Read about the dragon in Bel and the Dragon 1:23–27. Discover more about wrong worship in Revelation 13:1–4.]

(DANIEL, PART 2)

Daniel has destroyed Bel and killed the dragon, both objects of the Babylonian people's worship. And they're mad, boiling with anger.

A mob forms. They come to the king, accusing him of converting to Judaism. They demand he turn Daniel over to them. If the king refuses, they'll kill him and his family.

There's no reasoning with a mob—even for a king. He has no choice and hands Daniel over to them. They throw him into a pit of hungry lions.

This is Daniel's second encounter with a pit full of lions. The first time occurred when Darius was king. Then Daniel's foes attacked him for his steadfast devotion to God and maneuvered the king into feeding Daniel to the lions. God shut the lion's mouths, and Daniel emerged the next day, unharmed.

Possibly recalling that one day with the lions wasn't long enough to kill Daniel, this time his enemies give him a six-day sentence. The lions receive no food that day to make sure they'll devour Daniel.

But on the seventh day, King Cyrus discovers Daniel still very much alive, sitting among the hungry lions. He has Daniel removed and his detractors tossed in. The lions kill and eat them without delay. After all, they've not eaten a thing for seven days.

What's been our pit of lions? When have others persecuted us for staying true to God?

[Read about Daniel in Bel and the Dragon 1:28–42. Discover Daniel's first encounter with lions in Daniel 6:16–24.]

50: HABAKKUK

The prophet Habakkuk makes a brief appearance in the Apocrypha. It's most astounding—though not unprecedented.

Habakkuk is in Judea, going about his daily work. He's on his way with lunch to feed his workers harvesting in his field.

An angel shows up and says, "Take this food to Daniel. He's in a pit of lions in Babylon."

Habakkuk responds, "I've never been to Babylon and know nothing about a pit of lions."

Besides, with Babylon being hundreds of miles away, this is an unrealistic command. Or is it?

The angel grabs the prophet by the hair and whisks him off to Babylon with a rush of wind, stopping right above the pit of lions. Habakkuk calls down to Daniel and gives him lunch.

Daniel gets up and eats, while the angel returns Habakkuk home.

But this may not be the first time in Scripture a person is supernaturally transported. Obadiah believed God would do it with Elijah, and he later does. In the New Testament God does it with Philip.

Do we think God could supernaturally move us from one place to another today? How would we react if he did?

[Read about Habakkuk in Bel and the Dragon 1:33–39. Discover more about God transporting people in 1 Kings 18:11–12 and Acts 8:39–40.]

1 MACCABEES

First Maccabees possesses both historical and literary value. It's a book of stoic faith. It opens with details of the political scene and the military situation in Judea in the second century before Jesus.

The initial focus is on the military leadership and bold exploits of Judas Maccabeus (that is, the Maccabee). It also covers the feats of his four brothers: Eleazar, John, Jonathan, and Simon.

Like many books in the Bible—most notably Jeremiah—the Maccabees books do not unfold chronologically. The text often loops back in the timeline to prior events to add new content or reemphasize what already occurred. For example,

Alexander dies early in First Maccabees, but then shows up twenty-six more times.

The books of 1, 2, 3, and 4 Maccabees also contain names we're familiar with from Greek and Egyptian history. Sometimes, these references may be archetypes instead of literal. As mentioned in our introduction, this technique of using archetypes occurs throughout the Bible.

Also note that the years given in 1 and 2 Maccabees are from a different dating system and don't align with the Gregorian calendar we use today. The CEB estimates that 1 Maccabees covers 169–134 BC.

51: DARIUS

We've already encountered King Darius in the chapters on Belshazzar and Daniel. Like King Cyrus, many biblical mentions of Darius appear to establish a time frame for the surrounding text.

Much of what we know about Darius the Mede comes from the book of Daniel. The first time we hear of him is when he conquers Babylon and kills King Belshazzar.

Darius later plays a role in the repatriation of some of the exiled people to their homeland and helps them to rebuild.

Yet just as Darius seizes control by force, he loses control the same way to Alexander.

Though we might applaud Darius for helping

God's people return home and restore right worship, we must remember he's a fierce military leader who rules by force through the might of his army.

How should we react to a mostly bad person who does something good? Are we known for what we do that's good or what we've done that's bad?

[Read about King Darius in 1 Maccabees 1:1. Discover more about Darius in Ezra 6:1–15 and Daniel 5:31.]

52: ALEXANDER (6)

Alexander is the king of Greece and the son of Philip of Macedonia. He also leads a powerful army intent on conquest. He defeats King Darius of the Persians and the Medes, which significantly expands his rule.

Overall, Alexander's successful military campaigns conquer the known world, killing kings and plundering nations along the way. People revere him as the supreme ruler.

Yet he gets sick. He divides his kingdom among his chief military leaders. Then he dies in bed, having ruled for only twelve years.

For all his power, his military might couldn't save him. In the end, his kingdom didn't matter.

Do we trust Jesus to save us, or are we relying on something else? What kind of kingdom are we building?

[Read about Alexander in 1 Maccabees 1:1–7. Discover more about being saved in Romans 10:9.]

53: ANTIOCHUS (1)

Antiochus is a king in the book of First
Maccabees.

He conquers Jerusalem, kills many,
and plunders the city. Then he sets it on fire, takes
women and children prisoner, and makes it his
fortress. Next, he implements extreme actions to
make the remaining people turn from God and
adhere to his beliefs. He bans their religious practices, defiles the sanctuary, and prohibits circumci-
sion, killing those who disobey.

Intent on further conquest, Antiochus goes to
Elymais, a city in Persia, because of its vast trove of
silver and gold. He attacks the city to plunder it but
fails. He flees in disgrace. At this same time, he

learns that his general, Lysias, whom he left in Judah to deal with the revolt there, has also suffered a sound defeat.

Shaken, he falls ill with grief. Depression overtakes him.

He laments that he was once loved for his rule. But that all changed when he attacked and plundered Jerusalem. He ordered the people's destruction without good cause.

Antiochus is in distress, dying of bitter disappointment and far from home. Though he doesn't state it, he infers that his present misfortune stems from all the wrong he did to Jerusalem. It's as if God is punishing him for his sins.

Yet despite acknowledging his wrong actions, he does nothing to correct his errors. Though he's remorseful, he takes no steps to turn his life around.

He soon dies in his brokenness.

When our life doesn't go as hoped, do we look to see what we may have done wrong? Does our repentance result in a change in our behavior?

[Read about Antiochus in 1 Maccabees 1:29–64 and 1 Maccabees 6:1–17. Discover another king who recognizes his errors in 2 Chronicles 33:1–20.]

54: MATTATHIAS (1)

M attathias is a zealous priest and father of John, Simon, Judas, Eleazar, and Jonathan. Much of the events in the Maccabee books revolve around Mattathias and his family, notably Judas, also called Maccabeus.

Yet our story begins with Mattathias.

As a priest and leader among the people, the atrocities of Antiochus grieve him. He laments their situation. He and his sons tear their clothes and go into mourning.

The king's officers urge Mattathias to serve as a role model for the people by leading them to do as the king commanded and adopt Gentile practices. Mattathias refuses, and he does so loudly, pledging to stay true to their faith.

Yet when he finishes his public declaration, a defiant Jew comes forward to offer a sacrifice to Modein. In righteous fervor, Mattathias rushes forward and kills the man at the altar, as well as the king's officer standing there.

So begins the Jews' rebellion.

Mighty warriors rally to join him. In excess enthusiasm, they destroy the altars to other gods, forcibly circumcise the uncircumcised Jewish boys, and hunt arrogant people.

As the end of Mattathias's life nears, he draws his sons to him, reminding them of their many forefathers whom God rewarded for trusting him. He encourages them to be courageous and grow strong in the Law.

He appoints Simon, his second son, to lead the family when he's gone. To Judas Maccabeus, his third-born and a proven warrior, he assigns command of the army.

He tells them to rally around the Law and make the Gentiles pay for what they did. After blessing them, he dies. The people mourn his death.

How zealous are we for God? When have we wrongly gone too far, as Mattathias did?

[Read about Mattathias in 1 Maccabees 2. Discover another man with great zeal for God in Numbers 25:6–13.]

55: JOHN (7) (GADDI)

Of Mattathias's five boys, we know the least about John, also known as Gaddi. Though John is likely the oldest son, when on his deathbed, Mattathias doesn't tell him to lead the family or lead the army. These fall to Simon and Judas (1 Maccabees 2:65–66). John gets left out.

We only have one story about John.

Jonathan sends his brother John on a mission. It's not a military quest but more so a diplomatic one. John's task is to receive permission to store supplies with their friends, the Nabateans. But Jambri's family attacks John, captures him, and leaves with everything he has. We later learn that they killed John, and his brothers take revenge.

John fails in his only assignment and dies. This suggests Mattathias showed wisdom in not assigning John any responsibility.

How should we respond when it appears someone overlooked or dismissed us? When have we failed to complete an assigned task?

[Read about John in 1 Maccabees 9:35–42. Discover another overlooked person—albeit with a different outcome—in 1 Samuel 16:1–13.]

56: AZARIAH (25)

When Judas goes out to battle, he leaves some troops behind under the leadership of Azariah and Joseph. They hear of Judas's victories and grow jealous. They want to receive some glory too.

Going against Judas's command to wait, they order their troops to march against their enemy. They suffer a great defeat, losing two thousand men that day.

All this happened because they weren't content to do what Judas told them to do. They sought glory but realized shame. Two thousand men died because of their disobedience.

This is the last we hear of Azariah, suggesting

Judas removed him from leadership because he couldn't be trusted.

Are we content to serve in a mundane role as assigned, or will we push for more? Though not likely resulting in death, when has our leadership hurt those under our care?

[Read about Azariah in 1 Maccabees 5:56–61. Discover another leader who disobeyed in 1 Samuel 13:7–14.]

57: JUDAS (7) MACCABEUS

J udas is the third son of Mattathias. He's also called Maccabeus, as in Judas Maccabeus, and later Judas the Maccabee. Since Mattathias is a priest, this makes Judas (and his brothers) priests by birth. Yet we don't see Judas functioning as a typical priest but as a military leader, which his father commissioned him to do. And a most successful military leader he is.

We know two things about Judas, and both are significant.

First, he had proven himself as a powerful fighter. This shows his natural, God-given prowess, along with seasoned experience. So his father appointed him to this role. In this position, he emerges as an astute military strategist who depends on God for victory.

Second, he steadfastly follows the Law, adhering to it fully, perhaps better than anyone since the days of Moses. The Law was important to his father and is important to him too. This honors God.

Though Judas could have trusted in his abilities to win battles, he trusts in God instead.

As a result, we see God's blessing on Judas as he wins battle after battle against much larger forces and often with no loss of life in his troops. He and his men pray and fast before battle. He trusts God for protection and has a string of victories. The nations in the area fear Judas.

Judas then cleanses and rededicates the temple, restoring right worship under the Law.

Do we look to our own abilities or look to God for our success? How well do we do at praying and fasting before we act?

[Read about Judas Maccabeus in 1 Maccabees 3:1–26 and 42–60. Discover another leader who trusted God with his battle in 1 Samuel 14:6–15.]

58: LYSIAS

Philip is an advisor to King Antiochus. On his deathbed, Antiochus appoints Philip to rule after he dies and to guide his son (also called Antiochus), grooming him to become king in his father's stead (1 Maccabees 6:14–16).

Yet King Antiochus had already given the same charge to Lysias.

This produces conflict between Lysias and Philip. Lysias could yield to Philip as having received the more recent and final instructions from the king, but he does not. Lysias may wonder how he can continue to rule, either through Antiochus or without him. Or he may resent mentoring someone who will one day surpass him.

Regardless, a political struggle emerges between

Lysias and Philip. It turns into a military conflict, with Lysias defeating Philip.

We don't know if Philip intended to follow through on the king's instruction or not. But this is the last we hear of Philip, which is not the case with Lysias, or with Antiochus's son, Antiochus Epiphanes.

When have we caused needless conflict between two people? How have we responded when asked to groom someone for a job we wanted?

[Read about Lysias in 1 Maccabees 3:32–34 and 1 Maccabees 6:55–63. Discover another man— Jehoiada—who guides a young king in 2 Kings 11:2 to 2 Kings 12:2.]

59: ELEAZAR (9) (AVARAN)

Elephants appear in Scripture, all in the first three Maccabees books. At this point in history, large militaries use elephants in battle. Many of the accounts of combat report troop and cavalry strength, as well as the number of elephants, such as in 1 Maccabees 6:30.

Sadly, the elephants do not receive humane treatment. Yet their size and strength make for a formidable presence on the battlefield.

During one battle, Judas's brother Eleazar (also called Avaran) notices one elephant is taller than the rest and wears royal armor. He assumes the king must be on it.

Full of zeal, Eleazar rushes into the battle, headed straight toward the imposing elephant. He slays men to his right and left to reach the animal. When he gets to his target, he slides under the elephant and rams his spear into the beast's underbelly. The animal dies, falling on Eleazar and crushing him.

We don't know if the king was atop the elephant or what happened to him. But we do know this is one of the few times Judas loses in combat. His troops flee.

Though Eleazar gave his life in battle, his sacrifice was in vain. His side still lost.

When have we sacrificed something in vain? Knowing the outcome, would we still make the same decision?

[Read about Eleazar in 1 Maccabees 6:42–47. Discover another man who sacrificed himself, albeit with a different outcome, in Judges 16:26–30.]

60: PTOLEMY (1)

King Ptolemy of Egypt forms an uneasy alliance with King Alexander. But Ptolemy's overture is a ruse. He wants to take Alexander's kingdom and add it to his own, to rule both Egypt and Asia.

Through deceit, Ptolemy gains control of the coastal towns. He then seeks an alliance with King Demetrius. This allows him to focus on fighting Alexander without interference from Demetrius.

The armies of Ptolemy and Alexander face each other for battle. Ptolemy's imposing force causes Alexander to retreat.

Ptolemy accomplishes his mission. Yet three days later he dies.

Demetrius becomes the king in his place.

How far will we go to get what we want? When have we used deceit to achieve our goals?

[Read about Ptolemy in 1 Maccabees 10:51–58 and 1 Maccabees 11:1–19. Discover more about the folly of worldly pursuits in Luke 9:25.]

61: CLEOPATRA

The alliance King Ptolemy makes with King Alexander occurs when Ptolemy offers his daughter Cleopatra to Alexander in marriage. Though a common practice, this doesn't make it right or any less despicable.

But it gets worse.

When Ptolemy seeks to make an alliance with King Demetrius, he again uses his daughter to make it happen. He takes her away from Alexander and gives her to Demetrius.

Cleopatra has no say in her fate either time.

Her father uses her in an attempt to achieve his desire for power.

Though history has much to say about

Cleopatra, these two instances are all we know about her through Scripture.

When have we used someone to get what we wanted? How should we respond when someone tries to use us?

[Read about Cleopatra in 1 Maccabees 10:57–58 and 1 Maccabees 11:12. Discover another king who uses his daughters for his agenda in 1 Samuel 18:12–30.]

62: DEMETRIUS (4)

King Demetrius (4) is the son of King Demetrius (3). He succeeds his father, who died in battle. But his troops hate him.

Jonathan—presumably Judas's brother—reaches out to Demetrius for peace. He wins the king's favor, who esteems Jonathan and ends hostilities.

Later, when his people rebel against him, Demetrius asks Jonathan for help. Jonathan sends three thousand troops and quells the uprising.

Though Demetrius enjoys a time of peace, the size of his kingdom doesn't satisfy him. He wants more.

He marches out and invades Media. Arsaces,

the king of Persia and Media, sends his general into battle. The general defeats Demetrius's army and arrests him. Arsaces then puts Demetrius under guard.

Are we satisfied with what we have? Is it wrong to want more?

[Read about Demetrius in 1 Maccabees 11:8–53 and 1 Maccabees 14:1–3. Discover another king who foolishly went into battle in 2 Chronicles 35:20–24.]

63: JONATHAN (9) (APPHUS)

Judas has a string of stunning military victories against overwhelming forces. When faced with a similar formidable situation, his men advise he retreat and regroup. He dismisses their recommendation and leads his men into battle. Though they prevail for a time, Judas dies in battle and his remaining men flee. His brothers Jonathan (also called Apphus, 1 Maccabees 2:5) and Simon bury him (1 Maccabees 9:5–19).

Without a military leader, opposition arises, and the people are distressed. They come to Jonathan and ask him to replace his fallen brother. Jonathan agrees.

Jonathan continues his brother's legacy. His

strong military strategy and diplomatic competence lead the people well.

Though Jonathan's father, Mattathias, tapped Judas to lead the military, when the task falls to Jonathan, he performs equally well. Though it may mean his father underestimated his abilities, it's more likely that he honed his skills learning from his brother and working with him.

Should we seek leadership or wait to be asked? Who can we learn from?

[Read about Jonathan in 1 Maccabees 9:23–73. Discover how another man responds to leadership in Judges 4:4–10.]

64: SIMON (12) (THASSI)

Jonathan leads his troops well, and they enjoy many victories. The nations and rulers fear his power and give him their respect. Yet Jonathan trusts the promises made to him by Trypho—a former supporter of Alexander—and he ends up dying.

His brother Simon—the last of Mattathias's sons—sees the lack of leadership. His brothers all gave their lives to protect the Law God had called them to follow. He feels it would be wrong for him to seek an easier life and not continue what they started.

Though not asked to, Simon (also called Thassi) assumes leadership of the army.

His decisive move encourages the people and

renews their courage. They applaud him as their leader in place of Judas and Jonathan.

Simon leads several successful battles and then promotes his son, John, as commander over the entire army. Simon also becomes the high priest. This means he leads his people militarily and spiritually.

The land enjoys a time of peace.

When is it okay to assume leadership when we've been neither asked nor appointed? What can we do to bring about peace?

[Read about Simon in 1 Maccabees 13–14. Discover more about peace in Judges 3:10–12 and Matthew 5:9.]

65: MATTATHIAS (2) AND JUDAS (9)

Simon is the last of his five brothers. He has at least three sons: Mattathias (2), Judas (9), and John (9).

Mattathias is most likely named after his grandfather—his dad's dad. That's all we know about his background from Scripture.

Judas—not to be confused with his uncle, Judas Maccabeus—is wounded in battle, his only recorded combat.

Simon, along with his sons Mattathias and Judas, visit the area towns to assess their needs and help them. Their next stop is Jericho. A man—identified only as Abubus's son—welcomes them and throws an impressive banquet in their honor. But he's acting with deceit.

He gets Simon and his sons drunk. His men grab their weapons and kill all three. Though Simon accomplished much good during his life, leading both his family and the people well, Mattathias and Judas have little to show for their lives.

The direct lessons from this story are to not get drunk and be careful who you trust.

If we were to die today, what would we have to show for our lives? If we've not made the most of the life God has given us, what can we change?

[Read about Judas in 1 Maccabees 16:14–17. Discover a warning about being dulled by drinking in Luke 21:34.]

66: JOHN (9)

John is the son of Simon, grandson of Mattathias. Don't confuse this John with his uncle John (7) who was killed on a diplomatic mission.

As Simon ages, he passes command of the troops to his son, John.

After the murder of John's father and two brothers in Jericho, John becomes a target. But John learns of these plans and kills those who came to assassinate him.

Like his father, Simon, John achieves much. He fights battles, exhibits bravery, and builds walls for protection. He also serves as the high priest.

John leads the people well and does so with distinction. So concludes the book of 1 Maccabees.

Whether we lead or follow, do we do so with distinction? What traits of our parents should we emulate?

[Read about John in 1 Maccabees 13:53 and 1 Maccabees 16. Discover two leaders who did as their father did, one bad and one good in 1 Kings 15:3 and 1 Kings 22:43.]

2 MACCABEES

Though we might expect 2 Maccabees to pick up where 1 Maccabees ended, it does not. As already noted, the Maccabees books do not unfold chronologically. The CEB says 1 Maccabees covers 169–134 BC, whereas 2 Maccabees covers about 180–161 BC, not only overlapping some of 1 Maccabees but also beginning sooner.

In 1 Maccabees we said goodbye to all five of the brothers, the sons of Mattathias: John, Simon, Judas, Eleazar, and Jonathan. Yet they all show up in 2 Maccabees very much alive. This is especially the case with Judas Maccabeus, whom we will now encounter as Judas the Maccabee (that is, *the hammer*) in 2 Maccabees. Other characters (mostly malevolent ones) who died in 1 Maccabees also resurface in 2 Maccabees.

In 2 Maccabees, we read more stories about these people and see some repeats of events we already know about. This is because 2 Maccabees is written by a different author than 1 Maccabees and has a different point of view.

Since it's challenging—if not impossible—to form a coherent timeline through the text, don't try. It's best to embrace the many accounts in 2 Maccabees as individual lessons we can learn from and not as a holistic record that smoothly flows from start to finish.

As such, embrace 2 Maccabees for its narrative and don't focus on the details.

67: JASON OF CYRENE

Second Maccabees opens with two prayers and gives some context of the situation. Think of it as an introduction. Following it is a section labeled "Author's preface." This heading is not part of the original text, but a description added later. A better label, however, might be "Editor's Notes."

A group of unidentified editors have abridged 2 Maccabees from a voluminous five-scroll set, chronicling the stories of Judas the Maccabee and his brothers.

Jason of Cyrene researched and wrote these five scrolls. The editors of 2 Maccabees, accepting the accuracy of Jason's work, seek to condense his five-scroll opus into an accessible overview.

Without the initial meticulous work of Jason of Cyrene, we would not have 2 Maccabees today. Yet without the painstaking focus of the anonymous editors, 2 Maccabees would be much longer and arguably harder to read. Their efforts build upon the foundation Jason first established.

Thank you, Jason of Cyrene, for your work to bring about 2 Maccabees.

What are we doing today that others can build upon? What history should we record for the benefit of future generations?

[Read about Jason of Cyrene in 2 Maccabees 2:23–32. Discover more about building on the work of others in 1 Corinthians 3:5–14. Consider two other men from Cyrene in Luke 23:26 and Acts 13:1.]

68: SIMON (13)

Simon (13)—not to be confused with Simon (12), Judas Maccabee's brother—is not an honorable man.

Simon, from the tribe of Benjamin, receives an appointment to serve as temple administrator. Since we might rightly expect a priest or Levite to fill this position, Simon's selection likely comes from a government official—a non-Jew—and not from his people's leaders.

Regardless, Simon disagrees with Onias, the high priest, about how to manage the city market. Simon could defer to Onias's authority or at least seek a compromise, but he does not.

Instead, he escalates the situation by retaliating against Onias. He lies, submitting a false report to the governor that the treasury in Jerusalem overflows with unreported money that rightly belongs to the king.

In doing so, he makes trouble and causes problems for Onias and his people.

When the governor's representative doesn't seize the money and gives up, Simon resorts to slandering Onias. He lies that Onias threatened the representative and propagated malevolence.

Onias goes before the king—not to accuse Simon of lying—but to protect the temple and the welfare of the people.

Simon continues his opposition.

How should we react when others give a false report about our work for God? How should we respond when slandered?

[Read about Simon in 2 Maccabees 3:4–12 and 2 Maccabees 4:1–6. Discover other instances of false reports in Exodus 23:1, Matthew 26:59–61, Acts 6:8–14, and 1 Peter 3:16.]

69: HELIODORUS

After Simon submits his false report to the king about the stash of money in Jerusalem, the king sends his chief administrator, Heliodorus, to confiscate the money for the royal treasury. Heliodorus leaves at once.

Onias tells Heliodorus there is some money, but not nearly as much as Simon falsely claimed. And what money they have is for widows and orphans, effectively belonging to them. Heliodorus, however, refuses to budge. He sets the date when he will seize the funds for the king.

The priests and the people beg God for help. On their knees and with raised hands, they implore the Almighty to protect the money reserved for the widows and orphans.

As Heliodorus and his soldiers approach the treasury, God's supernatural power manifests. A horse and fearsome rider appear before them. The horse kicks Heliodorus with his front legs, knocking the bewildered man to the ground. Two men also appear on either side and pummel Heliodorus, rendering him unconscious.

His men carry him away. As he lies dying, his men beg Onias to intercede for Heliodorus. Fearing he'll receive the blame if Heliodorus dies, Onias offers a sacrifice for the fatally injured man.

The two men who attacked Heliodorus reappear. Instead of further afflicting him, however, they confirm that because of Onias's intercession, God will restore his life. In response, Heliodorus should tell everyone about God's great power. Then the two men disappear.

Heliodorus recovers and does as instructed, leaving Jerusalem without the money.

What can we learn about God's power from this story? How willing are we to tell others about what God has done in our lives?

[Read about Heliodorus in 2 Maccabees 3:6–40. Discover other supernatural manifestations in Numbers 22:28–33, 2 Kings 2:11–12, 2 Kings 6:15–17, and Daniel 3:22–25.]

70: MENELAUS

Though Heliodorus gives up trying to take the people's money for the king, their ordeal isn't over. As we covered, Simon (13) continues his opposition. Three years later, his schemes come to fruition.

Jason (5), whom we'll cover next, sends Simon's brother Menelaus to seize the funds. He has Onias killed. He also grants approval for the commission of sacrificial acts against Jerusalem, reportedly plundering the temple.

The people oppose Menelaus, charging him before the king in these matters. Without an ally to come to his defense, he buys his way out of the situation and is acquitted. He even has his accusers falsely condemned to die, adding to his depravity.

Through the greed of those in power, Menelaus remains in office and continues his evil conspiracy against the people.

How do we respond when confronted with injustice? How willing are we to stand up to corruption?

[Read about Menelaus in 2 Maccabees 4:23–50. Discover another man who tried to buy power in Acts 8:17–24.]

71: JASON (5)

There are three men named Jason in 1 and 2 Maccabees. The first two are noble. The third one, Jason (5), is not. Though he serves as high priest, he's a crooked one. Here is his story.

Jason becomes the high priest, not through lineage or merit but through corruption. Basically, he buys the position. As soon as he assumes his role as high priest, he makes the people adopt a Greek lifestyle, completely disregarding their Jewish heritage and the Law that Judas the Maccabee and his family fought to uphold.

In doing so, Jason leads the people astray. The text calls him "excessively wicked and ungodly."

Later, it adds he has the "temper of a cruel tyrant and the wrath of a savage beast."

He treats the loyal priests with contempt and neglects the prescribed sacrifices, promoting athletic games in their place. The people follow his push to embrace the Greek way of life.

But just as Jason bought the priesthood, Menelaus later outbids and replaces him. When Jason sees an opportunity to get noticed by the government leaders, he slaughters some of his own people. But instead of gaining the attention of those in charge, he earns the ire of the Jews.

Jason flees for his life and lives as a fugitive in exile. When he dies, no one cares. They don't mourn his passing or even give him a funeral.

When have we tried to buy what we should have earned? When have we done the wrong thing to get someone's attention?

[Read about Jason in 2 Maccabees 4:7–29 and 2 Maccabees 5:5–10. Discover other corrupt priests in Matthew 27:20.]

72: AURANUS

As part of Menelaus's assault against the Jewish people, he grants approval to Lysimachus to commit sacrilegious acts against the city. The crowds rally in opposition to Lysimachus because they believe he pilfered the temple's gold. (The text doesn't say if this is true or not.)

With a riot brewing, Lysimachus arms three thousand men—a cruel force—under the command of Auranus. The only verse about him in Scripture says he is as senseless as he is old. What a stinging rebuke of Auranus.

Though we don't want to criticize him for being old—for we all age—the context suggests he may be too old to lead with competence, with his best days behind him. In addition, he is full of folly. These traits reveal him as a poor choice as a leader, and we're left wondering why Lysimachus picked him.

Regardless, in the skirmish that follows, the people prevail. They wound many and kill some. The rest of the troops flee. They capture and kill Lysimachus.

The passage doesn't say what happens to Auranus, but since he's never mentioned again in Scripture, it's not a stretch to assume he also died in the conflict.

How would others characterize us? If we don't like the answer, what must we change?

[Read about Auranus in 2 Maccabees 4:39–42. Discover two other older men who contrast to Auranus in Deuteronomy 34:1–7 and Joshua 14:6–14.]

73: PHILIP (6)

King Antiochus appoints Philip as governor of Jerusalem. Philip is a barbarous man, even more so than the king who assigns him. This vicious characteristic, paralleling the king's, may be the very reason the king taps him to serve as governor.

The king determines to force the Jews to turn from their beliefs and practices. He defiles their temple. It becomes impossible for the people to keep the Sabbath or even profess to being Jewish.

Some people gather in secret, hiding in caverns, to observe the Sabbath. But someone tells Philip of their clandestine worship service. He has them burned alive.

In doing so, Philip proves his barbarism.

How far will we go to stay true to our faith? If worshiping God becomes prohibited, will we do so anyway?

[Read about Philip in 2 Maccabees 5:21–22 and 2 Maccabees 6:1–11. Discover other instances of being burned alive in Leviticus 10:1–2 and Judges 15:6.]

74: ANTIOCHUS EPIPHANES

Antiochus Epiphanes, sometimes shortened to Antiochus, is the son of King Antiochus. Before he dies, King Antiochus charges Lysias to raise his son and groom him to lead. He later asks Philip to do the same thing. The two men clash in a power struggle, with Lysias besting Philip.

Lysias renames Antiochus Epiphanes as Eupator (that is, Antiochus Eupator). We don't know how seriously Lysias works to prepare his charge to become king, but Antiochus does indeed ascend to the throne. When he does, he appoints Lysias as supreme governor.

Judas (also known as the Maccabee) recovers the

temple and Jerusalem, restoring right worship. They celebrate the Festival of Booths.

This marks the end of the rule of Antiochus Epiphanes over the area.

It's later reported that King Demetrius kills both Antiochus Epiphanes and Lysias (2 Maccabees 14:1–2).

If we have a mentor, how well do we receive instructions and follow them? How can we honor those who mentor us?

[Read about Antiochus Epiphanes in 1 Maccabees 1:10, 1 Maccabees 6:17, and 2 Maccabees 10:1–13. Discover advice from another mentor in 1 Timothy 4:12.]

75: NICANOR

Nicanor appears in 1 Maccabees, which records his death. But because of the overlapping timelines in the Maccabees books, Nicanor is alive in 2 Maccabees, where we read more about him and discover an interesting twist. Second Maccabees again records his death.

Nicanor is one of the king's most valued advisors and is chosen to attack and defeat Judas the Maccabee. With an army of 20,000, he sets out to annihilate all those in Judea. He promises to sell the Jewish prisoners of war into slavery to raise money for the king. He even invites one thousand merchants to his expected sale.

Yet Judas—with a much smaller army but

relying on God—prevails over Nicanor, killing nine thousand troops and wounding more. Nicanor retreats in humility, fleeing as a fugitive. He says the Jews can't be defeated because they follow God's laws. But his story doesn't end here.

A few years later, Nicanor brings another army against the Jews. Though Simon's contingent struggles against Nicanor, Judas's troops fight with bravery and courage, so much so that Nicanor grows afraid and proposes peace.

With a peace agreement in place, Nicanor lives for a time in Jerusalem and grows fond of Judas, enjoying cordial interactions. Yet, when Nicanor's peace treaty is questioned, he receives instructions to capture Judas. But Judas outwits Nicanor and escapes.

In a subsequent battle, Judas prevails with God's help, kills thirty-five thousand enemy soldiers, and defeats Nicanor, who dies.

Though Nicanor once respected Judas and proclaimed he'd done nothing wrong, Nicanor returns to opposing Judas and fighting against him.

Do we place our trust in what we can see (such as troop size) or in God, whom we can't see? Does following God's laws guarantee we won't face defeat?

[Read about Nicanor in 2 Maccabees 8:8–36, 2 Maccabees 14:11–36, and 2 Maccabees 15:25–35. Discover the story Judas mentions when encouraging his men in 2 Kings 19:32–37.]

76: RAZIS

Tucked inside the account of Nicanor, we have a story of Razis, who is denounced before Nicanor. Yet Razis emerges as a man of valor.

Razis is an elder of the people. They love him, speak well of him, and call him "Father of the Jews." This is because of his renowned kindness toward them. He'd already been on trial, risking his life for what he believed in.

Wanting to make a statement of his hatred for the Jews, Nicanor sends a contingent of five hundred soldiers to arrest the innocent Razis.

Razis flees to a tower and is about to be taken. He falls on his sword, wanting to die bravely rather than face capture and torture. Yet in his haste, he doesn't die, but he is badly wounded.

He runs to the wall and throws himself into the mob. But the mob pulls away, and he lands with a thud, still alive. In a rage, he climbs a pile of rubble and kills himself with his own hands and dies, calling out to God.

This passage of Razis's death is gruesome, yet we shouldn't focus on the gore of his demise but on his zeal for his God and his faith.

Are we known for our valor and zeal? How do we envision our death?

[Read about Razis in 2 Maccabees 14:37–46. Discover other men who take their own lives in 1 Samuel 31:3–5 and Matthew 27:3–5.]

1 ESDRAS

The book of 1 Esdras is essentially a carefully selected compilation of passages from 2 Chronicles, Ezra, and Nehemiah.

As such, it contains many familiar stories from those Old Testament books, as well as 2 Kings.

There is some naming confusion about this book, however, with some Bibles labeling the text as 3 Esdras, since they call the book of Ezra, 1 Esdras, and the book of Nehemiah, 2 Esdras.

Esdras is the Greek form of Ezra. Some Bible scholars assign authorship of 1 Esdras (along with 1 and 2 Chronicles, Ezra, Nehemiah, and 2 Esdras) to Ezra, the priest, prophet, and scribe.

First Esdras is not in all versions of the Apocrypha but is part of the Greek Orthodox and Slavonic Orthodox Bibles. Besides the CEB, it's also in some printings of the RSV, NRSV, and WYC (Wycliffe Bible), as well as the original KJV.

77: JOSIAH

Josiah is one of Judah's kings. In a rare exception from most of them, he stands out as a God-honoring ruler. Scripture celebrates three kings for staying true to God. They are David, Hezekiah, and Josiah (Sirach 49:4). All three are in Jesus's family tree.

Josiah appears most often in the book of 2 Kings, followed by 2 Chronicles. Third is 1 Esdras, with the book of Jeremiah close behind.

In 1 Esdras, we read two accounts of his life, which the author deems as the most important. The second one chronicles his death, resulting from his own poor decision and failure to listen.

The first—and most significant—is the story of Josiah's grand celebration of the Passover. This follows his wide-sweeping religious reforms to get the nation to return to their roots and again make God their priority.

It is an impressive observance that might strike us as excessive. But is anything too excessive when worshiping God? The text says no Passover was celebrated with such exuberance since the time of Samuel the prophet.

This means King Josiah's worship outshines all the kings who went before him, even King David and King Solomon.

Who might people compare us to? Has our worship of God ever faced criticism for being too excessive?

[Read about Josiah in 1 Esdras 1:1–31. Discover when David is criticized for his excessive worship in 2 Samuel 6:12–22.]

78: JEHOIAKIM

King Josiah implemented sweeping religious reforms and honored God. Yet his descendants do not follow his example. They have unworthy reigns. This starts with his son Jehoiakim, who replaces his father as king.

Jehoiakim ascends to the throne when he is twenty-five. He rules for eleven years. And he does what is evil in God's eyes.

That's all 1 Esdras says about him. And that's all we need to know. It's a sad legacy of disobeying God and rebelling against his laws.

Yet this disheartening characterization—of doing evil in God's eyes—repeats for many of the kings of Israel and Judah. Though they should learn from history, they do not.

How do we think God characterizes us? What do we need to change?

[Read about Jehoiakim in 1 Esdras 1:35–40. Discover more about Jehoiakim in 2 Kings 24:1–6.]

79: HILKIAH (11)

There are several men named Hilkiah in Scripture. Most receive scant mentions in the text. Such is the case with Hilkiah (11). He only appears once, and he's part of a list. Nevertheless, he provides a noteworthy example for us to consider.

Hilkiah is one of three chief officials of the temple during the reign of King Josiah. The other two are Zechariah (14) and Jehiel. This trio gives generously to the Passover celebration. Together they provide 2,600 sheep and 300 calves. That's a lot of animals, nearly three thousand, which averages to nearly one thousand each.

Since Hilkiah appears first in the list, we can assume he takes the lead in this donation, and he likely gives the most. This indicates he is a wealthy man. And he shares liberally from what God has given him to bless others.

Hilkiah and his two associates follow the example of King Josiah in providing animals for the Passover celebration. And several other men likewise follow Hilkiah's example with their own contributions.

After King Josiah, Hilkiah took the lead in contributing animals for Passover and set an example for others to follow. The result was a magnificent celebration.

How can we share our blessings from God to bless others? How can we better celebrate God?

[Read about Hilkiah in 1 Esdras 1:7–20 and 2 Chronicles 35:8. Discover another sizable animal sacrifice in 2 Chronicles 7:5.]

80: NEBUCHADNEZZAR

K ing Nebuchadnezzar is a familiar name in Scripture. He appears in eight Old Testament books, with Jeremiah and Daniel being the most prominent. He also shows up in six books of the Apocrypha, with Judith leading the way, followed by 1 Esdras.

First Esdras chronicles King Nebuchadnezzar conquering Judah and deporting many of its people. This event stands as a pivotal point for the nation of Judah. It marks the punishment God's rebellious people deserve. Though God showed remarkable patience and mercy over the centuries toward his people's repeated disobedience, his judgment finally arrives at the hand of Nebuchadnezzar.

Nebuchadnezzar first removes the evil King Jehoiakim from power and takes him to Babylon, along with some of God's holy items from the temple. Jehoiakim's son, Jehoiachin, rules Judah in place of his father, but only for a short time.

A year later, Nebuchadnezzar returns. He likewise hauls Jehoiachin off to Babylon, along with the rest of the holy items, treasure chests, and the royal stores. Nebuchadnezzar kills many of the people. He razes the temple, destroys the city walls, and burns its towers. Under guard, he deports the survivors to Babylon to serve him.

In doing so, Nebuchadnezzar fulfills the prophecy of Jeremiah.

Though Nebuchadnezzar accomplishes God's purpose in punishing Judah, this doesn't mean he has God's favor. He does not. God will later punish Nebuchadnezzar and all of Babylon for what they did to God's chosen people.

Though this may not seem fair to us in our finite minds, we must acknowledge that God is sovereign and can do whatever he wants.

What do we think about God using ungodly people to

accomplish his will? How can we better understand God's sovereignty?

[Read about Nebuchadnezzar in 1 Esdras 1:37–55. Discover more about Nebuchadnezzar in Jeremiah 25:8–14 and Jeremiah 52:4–30.]

81: ZEDEKIAH

Nebuchadnezzar removes Jehoiachin from power and sends him into exile, replacing him with Zedekiah.

Zedekiah assumes the throne when he is twenty-one. His reign lasts eleven years. Like his predecessors, he does evil before God and ignores the warnings of the prophet Jeremiah.

Serving as a puppet for Nebuchadnezzar, Zedekiah pledges to support the king. To confirm his intentions, Nebuchadnezzar has Zedekiah swear in the Lord's name. Yet Zedekiah doesn't honor his word and reneges on his promise. He rebels against Nebuchadnezzar.

Making an oath in God's name apparently carries more weight with the pagan

Nebuchadnezzar than with the Jewish Zedekiah. Even worse, Zedekiah rebels against God. Being stubborn, he breaks God's rules and doesn't follow him.

In what ways have we been stubborn against God? How have we rebelled?

[Read about Zedekiah in 1 Esdras 1:44–46. Discover more about Zedekiah in 2 Chronicles 36:11–16.]

82: SHESHBAZZAR

O ur story shifts forward some seventy years. As prophesied, King Nebuchadnezzar is gone and so is the Babylonian empire (Jeremiah 29:10–11). The Persian King Cyrus now rules. He decrees that the temple in Jerusalem should be rebuilt (2 Chronicles 36:23).

Cyrus retrieves the items of worship that Nebuchadnezzar pilfered from the temple. He entrusts them—5,469 gold and silver objects—to Sheshbazzar, a "prince of Judah" and later its governor. He is to use them to rebuild the temple.

Sheshbazzar and the exiles—also called prisoners of war—transport these items back to Jerusalem, where they belong. A subsequent text says that Zerubbabel (whom we'll cover next) is with Sheshbazzar.

Sheshbazzar safely returns to Jerusalem and begins to rebuild the temple. But he doesn't finish.

Do people trust us with critical assignments? What have we started but failed to finish?

[Read about Sheshbazzar in 1 Esdras 2:7–11 and 1 Esdras 6:12–19. Discover more about Sheshbazzar in Ezra 5:6–17.]

83: ZERUBBABEL

So far in 1 Esdras we've covered several people who—although offering us helpful insight—are incidental to the primary intent of the book: rebuilding the temple and restoring right worship. Zerubbabel helps make this happen.

Most of what we read in 1 Esdras comes from other books in the Bible. But this next story—an interesting aside—is not. It's Zerubbabel's back-story. Here's what happens.

Three young men serve as bodyguards to King Darius. We later learn that Zerubbabel is one of them. They devise a contest to see who is the wisest. Zerubbabel's answer supersedes those of the other two men and then builds upon them, proclaiming truth as above all else.

Declared the winner—the wisest of the three— King Darius tells Zerubbabel to ask whatever he wants, and the king will grant it.

Zerubbabel requests nothing for himself. Instead, he reminds the king of his promise to rebuild the temple in Jerusalem and begs him to complete that work. Darius agrees and commissions Zerubbabel to do so, providing letters of authorization to facilitate the process. Zerubbabel later becomes governor, implicitly replacing Sheshbazzar.

Though Zerubbabel didn't ask for permission to rebuild the temple, this is exactly what he received. In achieving this outcome, he proved his wisdom and revealed his strategic tact.

How do we show wisdom? Do we seek things for ourselves or to honor God?

[Read about Zerubbabel in 1 Esdras 4:13–61 and 1 Esdras 4:42–60. Discover more about gaining wisdom in James 1:5.]

84: JESHUA (3)

Jeshua is a priest who returns to Jerusalem along with Zerubbabel. The two often appear in tandem as leaders of the people who resettled there. Their pairing makes sense as Jeshua, a descendant of Aaron, is a leading priest, while Zerubbabel, a descendant of King David and therefore part of the royal line, serves as governor.

Though Zerubbabel usually appears before Jeshua, one time the order is reversed (1 Esdras 5:47). Regardless, they work together, with Jeshua as a spiritual leader and Zerubbabel as a political leader. Yet Zerubbabel likely takes the lead, with Jeshua being second to him.

There is one time, however, where Jeshua acts when Zerubbabel remains inactive.

Jeshua, along with his sons and associates, takes an active part in rebuilding the temple, while Zerubbabel does not.

Though Zerubbabel leads through his position, Jeshua leads by his example.

How well do we do in leading by example? When might it be appropriate for a leader to not take an active part in a project?

[Read about Jeshua in 1 Esdras 5:46–71. Discover more about when King David's men said he couldn't join them in battle anymore in 2 Samuel 21:15–17.]

85: NEHEMIAH

We've covered Zerubbabel and Jeshua, who serve as a one-two leadership team. One passage lists Nehemiah as the third leader, following the other two.

We know much about Nehemiah through the book named after him. Whereas Zerubbabel leads in rebuilding the temple, Nehemiah leads in rebuilding the wall around Jerusalem (Sirach 49:11–13).

Though Nehemiah is understandably central in the book of Nehemiah, he receives only a scant two mentions in the book of 1 Esdras. Apparently, the author of 1 Esdras considers the rebuilding of the temple as significant but not the rebuilding of the wall, since the text scarcely mentions its fallen condition and the need to rebuild it.

From a security standpoint, rebuilding the walls surrounding the city seems important—at least from a human perspective.

Yet 1 Esdras has a spiritual focus.

As such, the rebuilding of the temple and restoring proper worship stand as paramount concerns. Rebuilding the wall addresses a worldly fear and doesn't have direct spiritual implications.

Might the author's perspective—and our lesson —be that if we are right with God, he will protect us? The converse is that if we aren't right with God, nothing we do to protect ourselves will matter.

It's something to ponder.

When have we focused on physical needs instead of spiritual ones? Is it ever okay to trust God to provide without also following it with prudent action?

[Read about Nehemiah in 1 Esdras 5:8 and 40. Discover more about trusting in God in Proverbs 3:5–6.]

86: HAGGAI AND ZECHARIAH (15)

Haggai and Zechariah are contemporaries. They are also God's prophets during the leadership of Zerubbabel and Ezra. The messages of both prophets concern the importance of rebuilding the temple.

Haggai is the first prophet to emerge after the people of Judah return from their exile in Babylon. He focuses on the importance of the temple to the Jews. He urges them to make its reconstruction a priority. Haggai also criticizes their materialism and self-centeredness, instead of making God their focus.

Zechariah likewise calls the people to put God first, to return to him. A part of this is restoring proper worship in the temple. To do this, they must first rebuild it.

Though God's people too often ignore what his prophets say, this time is an exception. They listen. They do, indeed, rebuild the temple, albeit not without facing significant opposition.

Though Zerubbabel, Jeshua, and Ezra all play key roles in rebuilding the temple and restoring right worship, it all starts with the prophets Haggai and Zechariah.

What is God calling us to rebuild? In what ways does our worship of him need to be restored?

[Read about Haggai and Zechariah in 1 Esdras 6:1 and 1 Esdras 7:3. Discover more in Isaiah 58:12, Haggai 1:8, and Zechariah 6:15.]

PRAYER OF MANASSEH

Prayer of Manasseh records King Manasseh's petition to God mentioned in 2 Chronicles 33:12–13. It's a personal prayer of praise, confession, and seeking forgiveness. The central portion focuses on the king's passionate words of confession.

Although many recorded prayers of confession offered at this time in history address the sins of the people as a nation, Manasseh acknowledges his specific role in leading the people away from God.

We can read the Prayer of Manasseh as a psalm and use it to inform our praise and confession.

Prayer of Manasseh resembles David's repentant prayer of confession recorded in Psalm 51 about his remorse over his adultery with Bathsheba.

Prayer of Manasseh is not in most versions of the Apocrypha but is part of the Greek Orthodox and Slavonic Orthodox Bibles. Besides the CEB, it's also in some versions of the RSV, NRSV, and WYC (Wycliffe Bible), as well as the original KJV.

87: MANASSEH (2)

I n 2 Chronicles 33, we read the story of the evil King Manasseh, heralded by many as the wickedest of Judah's kings. In a time of distress, Manasseh seeks God and prays.

Though the book of 2 Chronicles doesn't record Manasseh's prayer, we can read it in the short, one-chapter book, Prayer of Manasseh.

This fifteen-verse prayer contains three parts. The first is praise. The second offers confession. And the third seeks forgiveness.

In the confession portion, Manasseh despairs over his own sins and pleads with God to forgive him. His words ring with remorse and reveal a repentant spirit.

God reacts to Manasseh's contrite attitude by restoring the king to power.

In response to receiving the Lord's forgiveness, King Manasseh undoes many of the wicked things he had done earlier in his life.

Regardless of the severity of the mistakes we've made, do we believe God can—and will—forgive us? How can we best respond to the mercy and forgiveness God gives us?

[Read Manasseh's request to God in Prayer of Manasseh 1. Discover more in 2 Kings 24:1–4 and 2 Chronicles 33.]

PSALM 151

Psalm 151 is an additional psalm not found in most Bibles.

Ascribed to King David, the text praises God for selecting him to become king and allowing him to defeat the Philistine warrior, likely Goliath (see 1 Samuel 17 for the complete story).

Psalm 151 is not in most versions of the Apocrypha, but it is part of the Greek Orthodox and Slavonic Orthodox Bibles. Besides the CEB, it's also in some versions of the RSV, NRSV, and WYC (Wycliffe Bible).

The CEB presents Psalm 151 as three related passages. Its first seven verses come from the

Hebrew text. The next two verses (whose source material is Syriac) serve as an addendum. Its final seven verses repeat the first seven, albeit from the Greek version.

The RSV and NRSV versions that include Psalm 151 provide only the main seven verses.

88: DAVID

As one of the best known and highly celebrated Old Testament characters, we know much about David, the shepherd boy who becomes king. Keeping all this in mind, we'll focus on what his own words in Psalm 151 reveal about himself.

First, David says he's the smallest of his brothers. This may refer to his size or perhaps it's a nod to his standing within his family. Recall that when Samuel went to anoint one of Jesse's sons, Jesse didn't even regard David as worthy of coming before the prophet.

Next, David acknowledges he's the youngest. He's the baby of the family, the last born. Yet even when delegated to the lowly position of shepherd, he sees himself as ruling over the sheep and lambs.

Third, he makes both a flute and a lyre so he can praise God. Praising God is exactly what he does in the middle of this psalm.

David ends by confirming that Samuel anointed him at God's direction. This made him leader over the people and ruler over God's children.

David started out ruling sheep and ended up ruling God's children.

He praises God for who he is and what the Lord did to make him king.

How do we view ourselves compared to our siblings? How might God's view of us contrast with our own?

[Read about David in Psalm 151 1:1–7. Discover more about David in 1 Samuel 16:1–13.]

3 MACCABEES

Three Maccabees is the shortest of the four Maccabees books. Historically, 3 Maccabees covers the time prior to the Maccabean revolt we read about in 1 and 2 Maccabees.

As a result, we won't see Judas and his four brothers in 3 Maccabees or encounter familiar characters we met in the first two books. Yet the text matches the theme of the other Maccabee books, with God saving his people from tyranny.

Taking place mostly in Alexandria, 3 Maccabees relates the Jewish people's harassment by the Egyptian king Ptolemy Philopator, circa the late 200s BC.

Third Maccabees isn't in most versions of the Apocrypha, but it is part of the Greek Orthodox and Slavonic Orthodox Bibles. Besides the CEB, it's also in some versions of the RSV and NRSV.

89: DOSITHEUS (1)

Dositheus is a cunning man, a Jew by birth who abandoned his people's customs and beliefs. In effect, he turned away from his faith.

He's with the Egyptian army, led by Ptolemy Philopator. When Theodotus plans to assassinate Ptolemy, thereby ending military conflict with a single targeted death, Dositheus leads Ptolemy away to protect him.

Dositheus arranges for an "unimportant man" to sleep in Ptolemy's tent. From a human standpoint, this man is not as important as the king, but we recognize that every life matters. We lament the dismissive label given to him.

Regardless, we don't know if this man realizes

he is standing in for the king and would become a target. Perhaps he assumes he'd received some honor, allowing him to sleep in the king's quarters. Or maybe this man volunteers for the assignment.

What we do know is that Dositheus uses this man, effectively sacrificing him to save the king. This is the man Theodotus kills. His death does not stop the war, but it does allow Ptolemy to live.

Had Dositheus remained true to his Jewish heritage, he would not have been in the Egyptian camp or been there to prevent the assassination of Ptolemy. In that case, the rest of the events in 3 Maccabees never would have occurred.

Is it justified to kill one person to stop a war and end its atrocities? Is it right to save the life of an evil person?

[Read about Dositheus in 3 Maccabees 1:3. Discover another man who abandons his faith in 2 Timothy 4:10.]

90: PTOLEMY (4) PHILOPATOR

Antiochus captures some of King Ptolemy Philopator's territory. The king wants it back. After surviving an assassination attempt, Ptolemy defeats Antiochus.

The Jews send a delegation to congratulate Ptolemy for his victory. He later travels to Jerusalem for a visit. He sees the brilliance and beauty of the temple and wants to enter the holy place (that is, the most holy place). They explain that only the high priest can enter and then only once a year.

In arrogance, Ptolemy thinks he's the exception and intends to go in. Despite their prayers and protests, he approaches the most holy place, determined to see what's inside.

What have we done in arrogance? When have we ignored the wise advice of others we should have listened to?

[Read about Ptolemy Philopator in 3 Maccabees 1:8–15 and 3 Maccabees 2:21–24. Discover others stricken by God in Numbers 12:10, 2 Kings 5:26–27, and Acts 13:11.]

91: SIMON (14)

With Ptolemy determined to enter the temple's most holy place, the priests prostrate themselves, and the people appeal to the Lord to stop the king from desecrating the temple.

The high priest, Simon, also kneels in front of the temple. He extends his hands and offers a prayer.

He praises God for stopping evil in the past, such as the great flood (Genesis 6:5–7), the wicked people of Sodom (Genesis 19:23–25), and Pharoah and his army (Exodus 14:26–31).

Interestingly, Simon never asks God to stop Ptolemy from doing what he intends to do, merely that God wouldn't hold them guilty for what he does. Simon ends by asking for mercy, grace, and the opportunity to praise God.

The Lord hears Simon's prayer.

God strikes Ptolemy with his judgment. He shakes the king like a reed buffeted in the wind. Ptolemy falls helpless to the ground, paralyzed and mute.

Seized with fear, his aides drag him away. The king later recovers from his ordeal, but his attitude doesn't change. He leaves, declaring vicious threats against the Jews.

What has God done to get our attention? When have we turned to him in distress and then pulled away when our situation improved?

[Read about Simon in 3 Maccabees 2:1–20. Discover another ruler who faces problems but doesn't change his attitude in Exodus 10:16–20.]

92: HERMON

Elephants only appear in 1, 2, and 3 Maccabees. They're used in military conflict. Ptolemy has a formidable herd of five hundred. Hermon is the keeper of the elephants.

Imagine the enormity and logistics of managing five hundred of these massive creatures. This is Hermon's job.

Wanting to kill the Jews and make a public sport for the people to watch, Ptolemy orders Hermon to drug the elephants and rile them up. He plans to have them trample the Jews the next morning as his people celebrate the Jews' destruction.

Hermon preps the elephants as ordered, while the Jews plead with God for deliverance. The next morning, the king oversleeps, sparing the Jews' destruction—for one day.

Ptolemy repeats his instructions to Hermon, who again readies the elephants to rampage the Jews. They petition God to rescue them again. The next morning, the king forgets he issued the command and reprimands Hermon. Again, this spares the Jews.

The king summons Hermon a third time, threatening him for insubordination and commanding him to equip the elephants to trample the Jews.

Though we'll hear of the elephants one more time in the book of 3 Maccabees, this is the last we hear of Hermon. He had faithfully obeyed the king's orders each time, yet he endured the king's wrath for the ruler's own shortcomings.

When have our leaders blamed us for their faults? How should we treat animals under our care?

[Read about Hermon in 3 Maccabees 5:1–38. Discover more about caring for animals in Exodus 23:12, and Proverbs 12:10.]

93: ELEAZAR (12)

After God rescued his people twice from being trampled by the raging elephants, the Jews are rounded up again. Chained and arrayed for death, the Jews cry and mourn. With their doom imminent, they give hugs and say tearful goodbyes.

Among them is Eleazar. He is a distinguished priest. An old man, he lived a lifetime of consistent virtue. Curiously, Eleazar stops the elders from praying, while he does.

In his petition, he remembers God's protection of the people from Pharaoh when they fled Egypt (Exodus 14:26–31) and later from the Assyrian King Sennacherib (2 Kings 19:35–37). He mentions Daniel's three friends in the blazing furnace (Daniel

3:23–27), Daniel in the pit of lions (Daniel 6:20–24), and Jonah in the fish's belly (Jonah 2:10).

In like manner, Eleazar asks God to deliver the people once again, and for the Gentiles to tremble at the Almighty's power.

When Eleazar finishes praying, two frightening angels descend from heaven to confront the forces opposed to the Jews. Thrown into confusion, the enemy freezes. The elephants turn around and stampede the army, trampling and destroying them.

God delivers the Jews for the third day in a row.

King Ptolemy witnesses it all. His anger toward the Jews turns to pity and remorse. He releases them from their chains and sends them to their homes, granting them their freedom. He orders a seven-day celebration in their honor, praising God.

How have we seen God supernaturally answer our prayers? Do we think God sends his angels to help and protect us?

[Read about Eleazar in 3 Maccabees 6:1–29. Discover other times foreign rulers praised God in Daniel 3:28, Daniel 4:37, and Daniel 6:25–27.]

2 ESDRAS

Unlike many other books of the Apocrypha, we know who wrote 2 Esdras: Ezra. Second Esdras takes place in Babylon, before Ezra returns to Jerusalem. This means that, chronologically, 2 Esdras occurs before 1 Esdras, as well as prior to the book of Ezra.

While much of 1 Esdras is *about* Ezra, 2 Esdras is written *by* him.

Ezra is the son of Seraiah (spelled *Saraiah* in the CEB). A multifaceted man, various passages describe him as a priest, a scribe, a legal expert (implicitly relating to Scripture), a reader of the Law, the chief priest, and a prophet.

It's his role as prophet that shines brightly in 2 Esdras. In 2 Esdras we see glimpses of other prophets in terms of style and content.

Ezra writes in first person, like Ezekiel and Daniel. He shares his angst, as do Jeremiah, Hosea, and Job. And he records visions, like many of the prophets, most notably Daniel, Isaiah, Zechariah, Ezekiel, and the apostle John. Second Esdras also records the prophet's prayers, as do the books of Jeremiah and Daniel.

Another interesting characteristic is that—as with the prophet Zechariah and the apostle John—Ezra interacts with angels. Most significantly, he engages with the angel Uriel, just like Daniel interacts with Gabriel and Tobias interacts with Raphael, also known as Azariah.

Last, 2 Esdras contains some of the most direct, forward-looking prophecies about God's Son—Jesus—of the prophetic Scriptures.

Second Esdras is not in most versions of the Apocrypha but is part of the Greek Orthodox and Slavonic Orthodox Bibles. Besides the CEB, it's also in some versions of the RSV and NRSV.

94: URIEL

The Lord speaks to Ezra, revealing truth and offering instruction. But Ezra struggles to understand what God means—as we all would. Ezra asks an angel to explain it. The angel's name is Uriel. Uriel talks to Ezra, just as the angel Gabriel instructed Daniel and later Zechariah.

Early in their conversation, Uriel asks if Ezra thinks he can understand God's ways.

Though this seems rhetorical, Ezra answers. "Yes."

Uriel asks Ezra if he can weigh fire, measure wind, or turn back time. Ezra, of course, cannot. Before long, Ezra realizes God's greatness and his own limitations. He falls to the ground and concludes he'd rather never been born than to not understand.

Ezra fasts and prays for seven days. His body shudders, and he faints. Uriel arrives to provide comfort, holding the prophet's hand.

Ezra fasts for seven more days and prays. Uriel and Ezra have a second discussion, which ends with the ground shaking.

Ezra weeps again and fasts for another seven days. His heart is disturbed, his spirit agitated, and his soul troubled. God speaks to him. Then Uriel arrives to give more instruction.

Throughout all this, Uriel has instilled patience in Ezra and gently guided him, bringing him to a place of being able to better hear from God.

Ezra is now ready for what happens next.

How should we react to the ways of God that we don't understand? What do we think about an angel holding our hand to comfort us in our deepest distress?

[Read about Uriel in 2 Esdras 4:1–20. Discover interactions with another angel in Daniel 8:15–22 and Luke 1:11–20.]

95: EZRA

While we read about Ezra in 1 Esdras —the book that mentions him most often—we can better learn about him from 2 Esdras, which he wrote. As autobiographical, we're treated to his thoughts as God reveals truth to him, both directly and through the angel Uriel.

Though we mostly know Ezra as a priest and spiritual leader who brings about religious reform in the book of Ezra, in 2 Esdras we get glimpses into his profoundly spiritual side as he strives to understand his interactions with God.

This book takes place in Babylon, assumedly before Ezra returns to Jerusalem.

The first thirteen chapters of 2 Esdras build up

—mostly guided by Uriel—to prepare Ezra for a greater revelation. This pinnacle occurs in chapter fourteen. (Treat the last two chapters of 2 Esdras as an addendum.)

In this revelation, the Lord comes to Ezra and speaks to him, as he did to Moses. This puts Ezra in good company, implying God esteems him just like Moses.

God says he will take Ezra from the earth to be with his Son. He will stay there—along with others just like him—until the end times. But before this happens, Ezra has some work to do.

He must warn the people—and he does. But he wonders who will warn those not yet born. God has a plan.

The Lord tells his prophet to gather writing tablets and five specific men who can write fast. For forty days, Ezra dictates what God supernaturally reveals to him through a holy spirit (or the Holy Spirit in the RSV). The scribes fill ninety-four scrolls. God also gives them an understanding of what it means, but they write in "characters" they do not know. (Consider Acts 2:4.)

The first twenty-four scrolls are for all the people now, both those who are worthy and those who are unworthy. The last seventy scrolls are reserved for those who are wise among his people.

How have we seen God work in us to prepare us for something greater? What should we write for those not yet born?

[Read about Ezra in 2 Esdras 14. Discover others God tells to write his words in Exodus 34:27, Jeremiah 30:2, and Revelation 1:19.]

96: MY SON

In one of Ezra's visions, he sees a woman in mourning. Infertile for thirty years, she at last gives birth to a boy. She calls him "my son." The mother delights in him and raises him. She finds a wife for him, but on his wedding night he dies (2 Esdras 9:43–10:1).

God reveals to Ezra that the woman represents the city of Zion, and the death of her son represents the destruction of Jerusalem (2 Esdras 10:40–49). Yet we can also see a secondary meaning, connecting this to Jesus's death (Luke 23:46) and marriage to us as his church (Revelation 21:2).

Beyond this indirect reference, through the woman's use of *my son*, God talks about *my Son*, meaning Jesus. He is the Son of God and expected Savior.

Here are four things 2 Esdras tells us about *my Son*.

First, he is the anointed one (2 Esdras 7:25–29). The context seems to reference Jesus's final coming we read about in Revelation 21:2, though it starts with him first coming to earth—as God's anointed one—to die in our place to save us (Acts 10:38–41).

Next, he will rescue those on the earth and judge the nations who rise against him and destroy them with fire (2 Esdras 13:27–38).

Third, no one can see him until his time is come (2 Esdras 13:51–52). We read about this in the four biographies of Jesus (Matthew 26:45, Mark 1:15, Luke 13:35, and John 12:23). His time came two thousand years ago, and it will come again in the future.

Fourth, Ezra will be with him (2 Esdras 14:9). In like manner, so will we (John 14:3 and 1 Thessalonians 4:17).

Do we believe Jesus is God's Son? How should we respond?

[Read about God's Son in 2 Esdras 2:46–48. Discover more about God's Son in Mark 1:1–3, Luke 1:35, John 5:25, and John 20:31.]

4 MACCABEES

Four Maccabees opens with a philosophical discussion on pursuing godly thinking to control our emotions and desires. The first three chapters are worth reading for the truth they contain, with the last three chapters serving as a concluding summary of the rest of the book.

The unidentified author builds his case using the examples of Joseph (Genesis 39:6–12), Dathan and Abiram (Numbers 16:1–35), Simeon and Levi (Genesis 34:25–31), and King David (2 Samuel 23:13–17) to illustrate the need to use our minds to control our emotions and desires.

He then moves the discussion to martyrdom

and being ready to die for our Lord, which clear thinking and self-control allow us to endure. He focuses on the martyrdom of nine people who are first mentioned in 2 Maccabees: Eleazar (2 Maccabees 6:18–31) and seven brothers and their mother (2 Maccabees 7).

In most of the rest of 4 Maccabees, the author significantly expands on the horrific details of their ordeal. Be warned that the graphic descriptions of abuse and torture in 4 Maccabees are some of the most intense in Scripture, but we'll not be that explicit here.

Four Maccabees is not in most versions of the Apocrypha, but the Greek Orthodox and Slavonic Orthodox Bibles include it. Besides the CEB, it's also in some versions of the RSV and NRSV.

97: ONIAS

We read about the high priest Onias in 1 and 2 Maccabees, who faithfully serves God and his people. Onias also appears here in 4 Maccabees.

Granted the title of high priest for life, Onias is both good and honorable, as we've seen evidenced in 1 and 2 Maccabees, which notes his devotion to God and hatred of evil (2 Maccabees 3:1). Another passage applauds him as virtuous, good, modest, gentle, and well-spoken (2 Maccabees 15:12).

Simon (13) opposes Onias and falsely accuses the high priest of various crimes. Unsuccessful in taking down his opponent, Simon enlists the help of Apollonius, claiming the temple treasury holds a vast amount of money, which rightly belongs to King Seleucus.

Under the king's authority, Apollonius goes to seize the stockpile but is nearly killed by supernatural forces. Fearing he'll be blamed if Apollonius dies, Onias prays for his healing. Apollonius recovers and leaves without the money.

The funds remain secure in the temple and Apollonius leaves a changed man, all because of the intervention and integrity of Onias.

Later, King Seleucus dies and his son, Antiochus Epiphanes, assumes the throne. He cancels Onias's appointment as high priest for life, giving it to Jason, who agrees to make an annual payment to the king for the position.

When have people made promises to us that were later broken? How did we respond to the disappointment?

[Read about Onias in 4 Maccabees 4:1–17. Discover other honorable people in 1 Kings 11:28 and Acts 17:11.]

98: APOLLONIUS (1)

Apollonius appears in both 1 and 2 Maccabees, as well as here in 4 Maccabees. He's in league with Simon (13) and opposes Onias and the Jewish people.

Simon tells Governor Apollonius there's wealth in the temple treasury that rightly belongs to the king. The king dispatches Apollonius to confiscate the money, and he moves in haste.

Apollonius and his armed soldiers approach the temple to seize the stash. God's supernatural power manifests. Angels on horseback arrive from heaven with flashing weapons. Apollonius and his men quake at the sight. He falls to the ground, half dead. Lifting his hands toward heaven, he begs the Jewish people to intervene and rescue him from the heavenly army. If he survives, he promises to tell everyone that God's divine favor protects his temple.

Apollonius's plea touches Onias. Fearing the king will assume Apollonius died at the hands of humans rather than God's, Onias offers a prayer for the suffering man. God delivers Apollonius from danger, and he tells the king everything.

Does this story sound familiar?

That's because this account of Apollonius parallels the passage about Heliodorus in 2 Maccabees 3:7–8. In that case, however, it is Heliodorus who leads the mission, albeit under Apollonius's direction. Though who suffered back then mattered to Apollonius and Heliodorus, it doesn't matter to us today which man God's supernatural manifestation confronted. The impact is the same, and the spiritual insights remain intact.

God supernaturally intervened to save his people and protect the temple treasury.

How do we react when we're mistaken for another person?

What about when we receive blame for what someone else did?

[Read about Apollonius in 4 Maccabees 4:1–14. Discover another man mistaken as someone else in Acts 21:37–39.]

99: ELEAZAR (13)

Eleazar is a priest, a legal expert, and ninety years old. He's rounded up when the tyrant Antiochus wants to force the Jews to eat pork, effectively renouncing their faith and turning from God.

The guards drag Eleazar forward to go first. They may reason that because of his old age, he'll quickly give in or that once he capitulates, the other people will follow his example. But Eleazar refuses to cooperate.

Some take pity on him and encourage him to escape torture and death by only pretending to eat pork. But he declines, rightly pointing out that others will see him eating and assume he ate the forbidden meat. They'll then be emboldened to eat pork and live because that's what he appeared to do.

To those of us today who don't follow Jewish dietary laws, it may seem as inconsequential to take one bite of pork and live. Yet to the Jews, obeying the Law was their path to God, standing as a salvation issue. Asking them to eat pork then would be like us being forced to denounce or curse Jesus today.

Just as many would willingly die today for their faith in Jesus, many back then would willingly die for their steadfast devotion to the Law.

Such is the case with Eleazar.

His refusal to eat pork brings about his torture and painful death. Yet he embraces the opportunity to die for what he believes in and serves as an example to others to stand firm.

What would we have done if we were in Eleazar's place? How can we serve as an example and encourage others to stay strong in their faith?

[Read about Eleazar in 2 Maccabees 6:18–31 and consider the expanded, more graphic, version in 4 Maccabees 6. Discover another man martyred for his faith in Acts 7:54–59.]

100: SEVEN BROTHERS AND THEIR MOTHER

Having failed to coerce Eleazar to submit to the king's demand and eat pork, Antiochus turns his attention to seven brothers and their mother.

One by one, each brother dies for his faith, enduring abuse, torture, and pain. They each stand firm—defiant even—in the face of unfathomable atrocities. They make bold declarations and encourage each other not to give in. Having witnessed the brutal suffering of each of her boys, the mother dies too.

The suffering and martyrdom of Eleazar, the seven brothers, and their mother provide potent examples of how to exercise self-control and not give in to the pull of our emotions and desires, even under the threat of martyrdom.

These people stood firm, even as they died a horrific death. This should encourage us to be self-controlled in the face of a temptation to sin.

Yet the torturous suffering they endured is nothing compared to what Jesus will later undergo. He willingly suffers and dies for the faults of all people, throughout all time, when he takes the weight of humanity's sins on his shoulders as he sacrifices himself on the cross to save us.

Thank you, Jesus, for who you are and what you did to make us right with the Father.

How have we suffered for our faith? How can we best respond to Jesus's suffering for us?

[Read about the seven brothers and their mother in 2 Maccabees 7 and consider the expanded, more graphic, version in 4 Maccabees 8–12. Discover others who suffered terrible atrocities for their faith in Hebrews 11:36–38.]

HEROES, HEAVIES, AND US

eroes and Heavies of the Apocrypha discusses some characters in a portion of Scripture that most people know little about. Some rise as heroes who—despite their shortcomings—can inspire us to do better. Others fail miserably. Yet they can show us traps to avoid and faults to rise above.

Both heroes and heavies fall short of our Lord's expectations.

But Jesus offers us a better way. When we repent and follow him, he makes us right with Father God. He wipes away the penalty our sins deserve and gives us a spotless record.

All we need to do is accept what Jesus offers. We don't need to change our behavior to gain God's attention or earn our salvation—we can't. It's impossible. Instead, God has prepared a no-strings-attached present that he graciously offers to us. We simply need to believe in the Lord Jesus (Acts 16:31).

In *response* we seek to change our behavior as a way of saying "thank you" to Jesus for the salvation he has given us.

May these characters of the Apocrypha inspire us to move forward in our faith journey with Jesus.

Here are some questions to consider:

- What character was the most inspiring?
- Which story was most surprising?
- What are some errors (sins) to repent from and stop doing?
- What are some errors (sins) to guard against?
- What are some characteristics of these people to celebrate?
- What are some characteristics to imitate?

Don't rush through them. Contemplate your answers. As you do, seek the Holy Spirit's guidance.

May God bless you as you read Scripture and

apply it to your life each day. May he receive your efforts as an act of worship, and may the world see your life as a powerful witness.

[Discover more in 2 Timothy 3:16–17].

If you liked *Heroes and Heavies of the Apocrypha,* please leave a review online. Your review will help others discover this book so they can read it too.

WHICH BOOK DO YOU WANT TO READ NEXT?

Other books in the Bible Character Sketches Series:

- *Women of the Bible*
- *The Friends and Foes of Jesus*
- *Old Testament Sinners and Saints*
- *More Old Testament Sinners and Saints*

For a list of all Peter's books, go to
PeterDeHaan.com/books.

ABOUT THE APOCRYPHA

Some versions of the Bible include the Apocrypha.

These are the Douay-Rheims 1899 American Edition (DRA), Good News Translation (GNT), New Revised Standard Version, Anglicised (NRSVA), New Revised Standard Version Updated Edition (NRSVUE), Revised Standard Version (RSV), Wycliffe Bible (WYC), The New Jerusalem Bible (NJB), New American Bible (NAB), World English Bible (WEB), and the Common English Bible (CEB), among others.

This book focuses on the text of the Common English Bible (CEB).

Note that some printings of the above Bibles may omit the apocryphal books, so get a complete,

unabridged version if you want to read it—or read
online, such as at BibleGateway.com.

DUPLICATE NAMES

Several people covered in this book share their names with other biblical characters. Sometimes these repeated names occur in the same family tree, where the name given to one child is in honor of someone in their lineage. For example, Abraham's grandfather is Nahor (1), and his brother is Nahor (2).

To avoid confusion, I've added a numerical suffix to distinguish duplicates. (Further complicating matters, some of these people also share names with cities or regions.)

Here are the names in this book which are shared with other people in the Bible. Though not always possible, I attempted to list them in chronological order, with the person we covered in italics.

Alexander

Alexander (1), a son of Simon who carries Jesus's cross (Mark 15:21)

Alexander (2), a member of the family of Annas, the high priest (Acts 4:6)

Alexander (3), a Jew in Ephesus who tries to quiet the crowd (Acts 19:33)

Alexander (4), a man whom Paul hands over to Satan to learn a lesson (1 Timothy 1:18–20)

Alexander (5), a craftsman who opposes Paul (2 Timothy 4:14)

Alexander (6), Philip's son who defeats Darius of the Persians and Medes (1 Maccabees 1:1)

Alexander (7), Alexander Epiphanes, a king and Antiochus's son (1 Maccabees 10:1)

possibly more *

Anna

Anna (1), a prophetess who praises God for Jesus's birth (Luke 2:36–38)

Anna (2), wife of Tobit and mother of Tobias (Tobit 1:20)

Antiochus

Antiochus (1), king and father of Antiochus (2) Epiphanes (1 Maccabees 1:10)

Antiochus (2), son of Antiochus (1); also known as Antiochus Epiphanes (1 Maccabees 1:10)

Antiochus (3), son of Alexander (1 Maccabees 11:39)

Antiochus (4), son of King Demetrius (1 Maccabees 15:1)

Antiochus (5), son of King Seleucus; also known as Antiochus Epiphanes (4 Maccabees 4:15)

possibly more *

Apollonius

Apollonius (1), governor of Coele-Syria and Phoenicia and son of Thraseas (2 Maccabees 3:5)

Apollonius (2), Menestheus's son (2 Maccabees 4:4)

Arphaxad

Arphaxad (1), the king of the Medes (Judith 1:1–5)

Arphaxad (2), an ancestor of Jesus and grandson of Noah (Luke 3:36)

Azariah

Azariah (1), a priest and grandfather of Azariah (2) (1 Chronicles 6:9–10)

Azariah (2), priest during the reign of King Solomon (1 Kings 4:2)

Azariah (3), overseer of Solomon's officials (1 Kings 4:5)

Azariah (4), a king of Judah (2 Kings 14:21)

Azariah (5), a close descendant of Judah (1 Chronicles 2:8)

Azariah (6), a distant descendant of Judah (1 Chronicles 2:38–39)

Azariah (7), a descendant of Azariah (1) and Azariah (2) (1 Chronicles 6:13–14)

Azariah (8), a Levite (1 Chronicles 6:33–38)

Azariah (9), a descendant of Benjamin and son of Azel (1 Chronicles 8:38)

Azariah (10), a priest who returns from exile in Babylon (1 Chronicles 9:10–11)

Azariah (11), a prophet during the reign of King Asa (2 Chronicles 15:8)

Azariah (12), a son of King Jehoshaphat (2 Chronicles 21:2)

Azariah (13) and (14), two priests who support Jehoiada in crowning young Jehoash king (2 Chronicles 23:1)

Azariah (15), a priest who confronts King Uzziah (2 Chronicles 26:17)

Azariah (16), a leader from Ephraim during the reign of King Ahaz (2 Chronicles 28:12)

Azariah (17) and (18), two Levites who support King Hezekiah (2 Chronicles 29:12)

Azariah (19), a chief priest (2 Chronicles 31:10)

Azariah (20) and (21), two priests who are ancestors of Ezra, possibly either could be one of the previously named priests (Ezra 7:1, 3)

Azariah (22), a man who helps repair the wall in Jerusalem (Nehemiah 3:23)

[There are five mentions of Azariah in the book of Nehemiah. They could be the same person, five different people, or somewhere in between.]

Azariah (23), one of Daniel's three friends (Daniel 1:6, Prayer of Azariah 1:1–2)

Azariah (24), the human name taken by the angel Raphael (Tobit 6:14)

Azariah (25), a leader who suffers defeat after disobeying Judas's instruction (1 Maccabees 5:56–61)

possibly more *

Baruch

Baruch (1), the scribe of Jeremiah and author of the book named after him (Jeremiah 36:4)

Baruch (2), a man who repairs some of the wall in Jerusalem (Nehemiah 3:20)

Baruch (3), a priest during the time of

Nehemiah (Nehemiah 10:6); he could be the same as Baruch (2)

Baruch (4), father of Maaseiah, a man who volunteers to live in Jerusalem, a descendant of Perez (Nehemiah 11:5–6)

Deborah

Deborah (1), Rebekah's nurse (Genesis 35:8)

Deborah (2), a judge (Judges 4:4–10)

Deborah (3), grandmother of Tobit (Tobit 1:8)

Demetrius

Demetrius (1), a silversmith (Acts 19:23–41)

Demetrius (2), a man highly esteemed (3 John 1:12)

Demetrius (3), son of Seleucus and king (1 Maccabees 7:1)

Demetrius (4), son of King Demetrius (3) (1 Maccabees 10:67)

Dositheus

Dositheus (1), a Jew who turns away from his faith and prevents the assassination of King Ptolemy (3 Maccabees 1:3)

Dositheus (2), a priest who preserves the letter of what Mordecai did (Greek Esther F:11)

Dositheus (3), one of the Maccabee's commanders (2 Maccabees 12:19)

Dositheus (4), one of Bacenor's men (2 Maccabees 12:35)

Eleazar

Eleazar (1), a son of Aaron and a priest (Exodus 28:1)

Eleazar (2), son of Abinadab who took care of the chest of the covenant (ark of the Lord) during the time of Samuel (1 Samuel 7:1)

Eleazar (3), one of David's mighty warriors (2 Samuel 23:9)

Eleazar (4), a Levite during the time of King David (1 Chronicles 23:21–22)

Eleazar (5), a man with a foreign wife during the time of Ezra (Ezra 10:25, 1 Esdras 9:26)

Eleazar (6), a priest who helps celebrate the completion of the wall in Jerusalem under Nehemiah (Nehemiah 12:42)

Eleazar (7), an ancestor of Jesus (Matthew 1:15)

Eleazar (8), father of Sirach (Sirach 50:27)

Eleazar (9), one of Mattathias's sons and brother of Judas Maccabeus; also called Avaran (1 Maccabees 2:2–5)

Eleazar (10), a leader of great learning during the time of Ezra (1 Esdras 8:43)

Eleazar (11), a man with a foreign wife during the time of Ezra, different from Eleazar (5) (1 Esdras 9:19)

Eleazar (12), a distinguished priest who prays and God shows his power (3 Maccabees 6:1–29)

Eleazar (13), a martyr for his faith (2 Maccabees 6:18 and 4 Maccabees 5–7)

Gabael

Gabael (1), an ancestor of Tobit (Tobit 1:1)

Gabael (2), the man who holds silver for Tobit (Tobit 1:14)

Hilkiah

Hilkiah (1), a Levite during the time of King David (1 Chronicles 6:45)

Hilkiah (2), a gatekeeper and one of Shimri's sons during the reign of King David (1 Chronicles 26:10–12)

Hilkiah (3), son of Eliakim and palace administrator during King Hezekiah's reign (2 Kings 18:37)

Hilkiah (4), high priest who discovers the instruction scroll in the temple when Josiah was king (2 Kings 22:8 and possibly 1 Chronicles 6:13)

Hilkiah (5), father of Eliakim (Isaiah 22:20)

Hilkiah (6), an ancestor of Ezra (Ezra 7:1)

Hilkiah (7), father of Jeremiah (Jeremiah 1:1)

Hilkiah (8), father of Gemariah (Jeremiah 29:3)

Hilkiah (9), a man who stands with Ezra (Nehemiah 8:4)

Hilkiah (10), an ancestor of Judith (Judith 8:1)

Hilkiah (11), a chief temple official during the reign of King Josiah (1 Esdras 1:8)

Hilkiah (12), an ancestor of Baruch (Baruch 1:1)

Hilkiah (13), father of the priest Jehoiakim, who receives gifts from the exiles in Babylon (Baruch 1:7)

Hilkiah (14), the father of Susanna (Susanna 1:29)

possibly more *

Jason

Jason (1), an ally of Paul's in Thessalonica (Acts 17:5–9)

Jason (2), a relative of Paul (1), possibly Jason (1) (Romans 16:21)

Jason (3), a son of Eleazar, sent on a diplomatic mission to Rome (1 Maccabees 8:17)

Jason (4), a man from Cyrene who records what happens (2 Maccabees 2:23–24)

Jason (5), a corrupt high priest and brother of Onias (2 Maccabees 4:7)

Jeshua

Jeshua (1), a priest during the time of King David (1 Chronicles 24:11)

Jeshua (2), a man, possibly a Levite, during the reign of King Hezekiah (2 Chronicles 31:15)

Jeshua (3), Jozadak's son and a leader who returned to Jerusalem from Babylon (1 Esdras 5:5–8)

Jeshua (4), a Levite during the time of Ezra (1 Esdras 9:48)

possibly more *

Jesus

Jesus (1), the star of the Bible and Savior of the world (every book in the New Testament)

Jesus (2), also known as Justus (Colossians 4:11)

Jesus (3), a grandfather of Sirach (Sirach Prologue:7)

Jesus (4), a son of Sirach (Sirach 50:27)

Joakim

Joakim (1), a rich man and father of Susanna (Susanna 1:1–4)

Joakim (2), a man who returns from captivity and the son of Zerubbabel (1 Esdras 5:5)

Joakim (3), the high priest during the time of Judith (Judith 4:6)

John

John (1), the Baptist (Luke 9:9)

John (2), one of Jesus's twelve disciples (Matthew 10:2–4)

John (3), father of Simon Peter (John 21:15)

John (4), a member of Annas's family (Acts 4:6)

John (5), also known as John Mark or just Mark (Acts 12:25)

John (6), father of Mattathias (1 Maccabees 2:1)

John (7), a son of Mattathias (1 Maccabees 2:2)

John (8), father of Eupolemus (1 Maccabees 8:17 and 2 Maccabees 4:11)

John (9), son of Simon (12) (1 Maccabees 13:53)

John (10), a man named in a letter; he could be John (7), John (8), or someone different (2 Maccabees 11:17)

Jonathan

Jonathan (1), a priest, the son of Gershom (Judges 18:30)

Jonathan (2), a descendant of Judah (1 Chronicles 2:32)

Jonathan (3), son of King Saul and friend of David (1 Samuel 14:1)

Jonathan (4), one of David's mighty warriors and the son of Shagee (1 Chronicles 11:34)

Jonathan (5), David's nephew, who kills a large man (1 Chronicles 20:6–7)

Jonathan (6), the son of Uzziah, who oversees some of the king's storehouses (1 Chronicles 27:25)

Jonathan (7), David's uncle (1 Chronicles 27:32)

Jonathan (8), son of Abiathar the priest (1 Kings 1:42)

Jonathan (9), priest and military leader; son of Mattathias and brother of Judas (7); also called Apphus (1 Maccabees 2:4–6)

Jonathan (10), father of Obed, from the family of Adin (1 Esdras 8:32)

Jonathan (11), son of Asahel (1 Esdras 9:14)

Judas

Judas (1), a disciple of Jesus and his betrayer (Matthew 27:3–5)

Judas (2), a half-brother of Jesus (Matthew 13:55)

Judas (3), the son of James (Acts 1:13)

Judas (4), a Galilean and rebel leader (Acts 5:37)

Judas (5), who lives on Straight Street (Acts 9:11)

Judas (6), also called Barsabbas and an esteemed person in the early church (Acts 15:22)

Judas (7), also known as Maccabeus, Judas

Maccabeus, or Judas the Maccabee; the son of Mattathias and a successful military leader (1 Maccabees 2:66)

Judas (8), son of Chalphi (1 Maccabees 11:70)

Judas (9), son of Simon (12) (1 Maccabees 16:14)

Judith

Judith (1), one of Esau's wives (Genesis 26:34)

Judith (2), a widow and hero who saves her people from annihilation (Judith 16:21–25)

Manasseh

Manasseh (1), Joseph's oldest son (Genesis 41:51)

Manasseh (2), king of Judah (2 Kings 20:21)

Manasseh (3), a priest with a foreign wife during the time of Ezra (Ezra 10:30)

Manasseh (4), another priest with a foreign wife during the time of Ezra (Ezra 10:33)

Manasseh (5), husband of Judith (Judith 8:1–3)

Manasseh (6), an Israelite with a foreign wife during the time of Ezra (1 Esdras 9:33)

Mattathias

Mattathias (1), a zealous priest and father of John, Simon, Judas, Eleazar, and Jonathan (1 Maccabees 2:1 & 24)

Mattathias (2), son of Simon (1 Maccabees 16:14–16)

Mattathias (3), an emissary of commander Nicanor under King Demetrius (2 Maccabees 14:29)

Mordecai

Mordecai (1), cousin and guardian of Esther (Esther 2:7 and Greek Esther 2:7)

Mordecai (2), a man who returns to Jerusalem with Zerubbabel (Ezra 2:2)

Nehemiah

Nehemiah (1), governor who rebuilds the wall around Jerusalem (Nehemiah 8:9)

Nehemiah (2), a man who offers sacrifices during the time of Judas the Maccabee (2 Maccabees 1:18)

Philip

Philip (1), disciple of Jesus (Mark 3:16–19)

Philip (2), brother of King Herod (Matthew 14:3)

Philip (3), a deacon in the early church (Acts 6:3–6)

Philip (4), father of Alexander (1 Maccabees

1:1)

Philip (5), named by King Antiochus to rule after his death and guide his son to replace him (1 Maccabees 6:14–16)

Philip (6), a barbarian assigned by Antiochus to govern Jerusalem, possibly the same as Philip (5) (2 Maccabees 5:21–22)

possibly more *

Ptolemy

Ptolemy (1), a king of Egypt (1 Maccabees 1:18)

Ptolemy (2), son of Dorymenes and advisor to King Antiochus (1 Maccabees 3:38)

Ptolemy (3), Abubus's son and governor over Jericho (1 Maccabees 16:11)

Ptolemy (4), also known as Ptolemy Philometor, king of Egypt (2 Maccabees 4:21)

possibly more *

Raguel

Raguel (1), an ancestor of Tobit (Tobit 1:1)

Raguel (2), father of Sarah (Tobit 3:7)

Sarah

Sarah (1), wife of Abraham (Genesis 17:15)

Sarah (2), wife of Tobias (Tobit 7:12)

Simon

Simon (1), a disciple, also called Peter, as in Simon Peter (Matthew 4:18)

Simon (2), a Zealot and another disciple (Matthew 10:4)

Simon (3), a half-brother of Jesus (Matthew 13:55)

Simon (4), the leper and the owner of the home where a woman anoints Jesus's head with oil (Mark 14:3)

Simon (5), a Pharisee and owner of the home where a woman washes Jesus's feet with perfume, though this could arguably be Simon (4) (Luke 7:39–50)

Simon (6), from Cyrene and who carries Jesus's cross (Luke 23:26)

Simon (7), Simon Iscariot, father of Judas Iscariot (John 13:2)

Simon (8), the sorcerer who asks to buy Holy Spirit power (Acts 8:9–25)

Simon (9), the tanner in Joppa, whom Peter stays with when Cornelius sends for him (Acts 10:32)

Simon (10), a man with a foreign wife during the time of Ezra (1 Esdras 9:32)

Simon (11), a great high priest (Sirach 50:1)

Simon (12), also called Thassi; son of Mattathias, brother of Judas, and his family's leader (1 Maccabees 2:1–5 and 1 Maccabees 2:65)

Simon (13), a temple administrator (2 Maccabees 3:4 and 4 Maccabees 4:1)

Simon (14), a high priest in Jerusalem when Ptolemy visits (3 Maccabees 2:1)

Uzziah

Uzziah (1), a king of Judah (2 Kings 15:13)

Uzziah (2), a descendant of Levi (1 Chronicles 6:24)

Uzziah (3), father of Jonathan (1 Chronicles 27:25)

Uzziah (4), a priest with a foreign wife during the time of Ezra (Ezra 10:21)

Uzziah (5), father of Athaiah and son of Zechariah around the time of Ezra (Nehemiah 11:4)

Uzziah (6), an ancestor of Ezra and descendant of Aaron (2 Esdras 1:1–3)

Uzziah (7), an elder in the town of Bethulia during the time of Judith (Judith 6:15)

Zechariah

Zechariah (1), king of Israel (2 Kings 14:29)

Zechariah (2), a descendant of Reuben (1 Chronicles 5:7–8)

Zechariah (3), a gatekeeper and son of Meshelemiah (1 Chronicles 9:21 and 1 Chronicles 26:1–2)

Zechariah (4), a descendant of Saul (1 Chronicles 9:37 and possibly 1 Chronicles 15:18)

Zechariah (5), a musician (1 Chronicles 15:20)

Zechariah (6), a priest (1 Chronicles 15:24)

Zechariah (7), a Levite during the time of King David (1 Chronicles 16:5)

Zechariah (8), another gatekeeper and son of Hosah (1 Chronicles 26:10–11)

Zechariah (9), a third gatekeeper, a wise counselor, and son of Shelemiah (1 Chronicles 26:14)

Zechariah (10), father of Iddo during the time of King David (1 Chronicles 27:21)

Zechariah (11), an official of King Jehoshaphat (2 Chronicles 17:7) and possibly his son (2 Chronicles 21:2)

Zechariah (12), son of Jehoiada, the priest (2 Chronicles 24:20)

Zechariah (13), father of Abijah (2 Chronicles 29:1)

Zechariah (14), an official of King Josiah (2 Chronicles 35:8)

Zechariah (15), the prophet and a descendant of Iddo (Ezra 5:1, the book of Zechariah, and possibly Ezra 8:3)

Zechariah (16), a priest guilty of marrying a foreign woman (Ezra 10:26)

Zechariah (17), son of Amariah and father of Uzziah (Nehemiah 11:4)

Zechariah (18), father of Joiarib and descendant of Zechariah (16) (Nehemiah 11:5)

Zechariah (19), son of Jonathan (Nehemiah 12:35)

Zechariah (20), a reliable witness and son of Jeberekiah/Jeberechiah (Isaiah 8:2)

Zechariah (21), son of Berekiah/Barachiah, murdered between the temple and the altar (Matthew 23:35)

Zechariah (22), the husband of Elizabeth and father of John the Baptist (Luke 1:5–25 and Luke 1:57–66)

Zechariah (23), father of Joseph during the time of Judas (7) Maccabeus (1 Maccabees 5:18)

Zechariah (24), a leader from the family of Parosh, who returns with Ezra to Judea with 150 men (1 Esdras 8:30)

Zechariah (25), a leader from the family of Bebai, who returns with Ezra to Judea with 28 men (1 Esdras 8:37)

Zechariah (26), a leader of great learning
(1 Esdras 8:43)

[With the number of obscure mentions of
Zechariah throughout the Bible—fifty-nine times in
nine books (plus more in the Apocrypha)—it's
impossible to determine accurately how many there
are. This list is reasonable but not absolute. The
main ones are Zechariah (1), king of Israel;
Zechariah (15), the prophet; and Zechariah (22),
father of John the Baptist.]

* There are possibly more men in the Apocrypha
bearing this name, but with the overlapping timelines and repetition—especially in the Maccabee
books—it's not possible to determine accurately if
there are more people with this name.

FOR SMALL GROUPS, SUNDAY SCHOOLS, AND CLASSES

Heroes and Heavies of the Apocrypha makes an ideal discussion guide for small groups, Sunday schools, and classes. In preparation for the conversation, read and think about the assigned chapters of this book each week.

When you get together, discuss the questions at the end of each chapter. The leader can either use all the questions to guide your conversation or pick some to focus on.

Before beginning your discussion, pray as a group. Ask for Holy Spirit insight and clarity.

As you contemplate each chapter's questions:

- Look for errors to correct (that is, sins to confess and avoid).

- Consider unwise behaviors and thoughts
  you should stop.
- Identify God-honoring actions and
  attitudes you can aspire to.
- Celebrate areas of success and strength
  to encourage yourself to persevere.

May God speak to you as you use this book to study
his Word and grow closer to him.

IF YOU'RE NEW TO THE BIBLE

Each entry in this book contains Bible references. These can guide you if you want to learn more. If you're not familiar with the Bible, here's a brief overview to get you started, give some context, and minimize confusion.

First, the Bible is a collection of works written by various authors over several centuries. Think of the Bible as a diverse anthology of godly communication. It contains historical accounts, poetry, songs, letters of instruction and encouragement, messages from God sent through his representatives, and prophecies.

Most versions of the Bible have sixty-six books grouped into two sections: The Old Testament and the New Testament. The Old Testament contains thirty-nine books that precede and anticipate Jesus. The New Testament includes twenty-seven books and covers Jesus's life and the work of his followers.

The reference notations in the Bible, such as Romans 3:23, are analogous to line numbers in a Shakespearean play. They serve as a study aid. Since the Bible is much longer and more complex than a play, its reference notations are more involved.

As already mentioned, the Bible is an amalgam of books, or sections, such as Genesis, Psalms, John, Acts, or 1 Peter. These are the names given to them, over time, based on the piece's author, audience, or purpose.

In the 1200s, each book was divided into chapters, such as Acts 2 or Psalm 23. In the 1500s, the chapters were further subdivided into verses, such as John 3:16. Let's use this as an example.

The name of the book (John) appears first, followed by the chapter number (3), a colon, and then the verse number (16). Sometimes called a chapter-verse reference notation, this helps people quickly find a specific text regardless of their version of the Bible.

Although the goal was to place these chapter and verse divisions at logical breaks, they sometimes seem arbitrary. Therefore, it's a good practice to read what precedes and follows each passage you're studying since the text before or after it may contain relevant insight into the portion you're exploring.

Here's how to look up a specific passage in the Bible based on its reference: Most Bibles contain a table of contents, which gives the page number for the beginning of each book. Start there. Locate the book you want to read, and turn to that page. Then flip forward to the chapter you want. Last, skim that chapter to locate the specific verse.

If you want to read online, enter the reference into BibleGateway.com or BibleHub.com. Also check out the YouVersion app.

Learn more about the greatest book ever written at ABibleADay.com, which provides a Bible blog, summaries of the books of the Bible, a dictionary of Bible terms, Bible reading plans, and other resources.

ABOUT PETER DEHAAN

Peter DeHaan, PhD, wants to change the world one word at a time. His books and blog posts discuss God, the Bible, and church, geared toward spiritual seekers and church dropouts. Many people feel church has let them down, and Peter seeks to encourage them as they search for a place to belong.

But he's not afraid to ask tough questions or make religious people squirm. He's not trying to be provocative. Instead, he seeks truth, even if it makes people uncomfortable. Peter urges Christians to push past the status quo and reexamine how they practice their faith in every part of their lives.

Peter earned his doctorate, awarded with high distinction, from Trinity College of the Bible and Theological Seminary. He lives with his wife in beautiful Southwest Michigan and wrangles crossword puzzles in his spare time.

Peter's a lifelong student of Scripture. He wrote the 1,000-page website ABibleADay.com to encourage people to explore the Bible, the greatest book ever written. His popular blog addresses biblical Christianity to build a faith that matters.

Read his blog, sign up for his newsletter, and learn more at PeterDeHaan.com.

PETER DEHAAN'S BOOKS

Bible Character Sketches Series:

Women of the Bible

The Friends and Foes of Jesus

Old Testament Sinners and Saints

More Old Testament Sinners and Saints

Holiday Celebration Devotional Series:

The Advent of Jesus (an Advent devotional)

The Ministry of Jesus (an Ordinary Time devotional)

The Passion of Jesus (a Lenten devotional)

The Victory of Jesus (an Easter devotional)

40–Day Bible Study Series:

Dear Theophilus (the Gospel of Luke, formerly That You May Know)

Dear Theophilus, Acts (formerly Tongues of Fire)

Dear Theophilus, Isaiah (formerly For Unto Us)

Dear Theophilus, Minor Prophets (formerly Return to Me)

Dear Theophilus, Job (formerly I Hope in Him)

Living Water (John)

Love Is Patient (1 and 2 Corinthians)

A New Heaven and a New Earth (Revelation)

Love One Another (1, 2, and 3 John)

Run with Perseverance (Hebrews)

Visiting Churches Series:

Shopping for Church

Visiting Online Church

52 Churches

The 52 Churches Workbook

More Than 52 Churches

The More Than 52 Churches Workbook

Other Books:

Jesus's Broken Church

Martin Luther's 95 Theses

The Christian Church's LGBTQ Failure

Bridging the Sacred-Secular Divide

Beyond Psalm 150

How Big Is Your Tent?

For the latest list of all Peter's books, go to PeterDeHaan.com/books.